THE PARADOX OF
INTERNET GROUPS

NEW INTERNATIONAL LIBRARY OF GROUP ANALYSIS

Series Editor: Earl Hopper

Other titles in the Series

THE PARADOX OF INTERNET GROUPS

Alone in the Presence of Virtual Others

Haim Weinberg

KARNAC

First published in 2014 by
Karnac Books Ltd
118 Finchley Road, London NW3 5HT

British Library Cataloguing in Publication Data

A C.I.P. for this book is available from the British Library

ISBN 978 1 85575 893 3

Edited, designed and produced by The Studio Publishing Services Ltd
www.publishingservicesuk.co.uk
e-mail: studio@publishingservicesuk.co.uk

Printed in Great Britain

www.karnacbooks.com

CONTENTS

ACKNOWLEDGEMENTS

Thanks to Earl Hopper for his helpful comments and to Miriam Iosupovici for her editing.

ABOUT THE AUTHOR

Haim Weinberg, PhD, is a Californian and Israeli licensed clinical psychologist, a group analyst, and a certified group psychotherapist, who moved to California, in 2006. For the past thirty years he has worked as a clinical psychologist, providing individual, couple, family, and group psychotherapy, as well as supervising interns and junior psychologists. He teaches at the Wright Institute, Berkeley, and the Alliant International University, Sacramento, as well as directing a group psychotherapy doctoral programme at the Professional School of Psychology, Sacramento. He is a past president of the Israeli Group Psychotherapy Association, and he is Fellow member of The American Group Psychotherapy Association (AGPA), Fellow of the International Association of Group Psychotherapy (IAGP), Distinguished Fellow of the Israeli Association of Group therapy, and member of the Group Analytic Society (GAS).

Haim Weinberg has published more than thirty papers and co-edited a book on the large group. He is now co-editing a series of books on the social unconscious, one of the volumes has been published already. Since 1995 he has been moderating the group psychotherapy discussion list on the Internet. Haim completed his PhD studies in the Manchester Metropolitan University about groups, their cultures, and the Internet unconscious.

For

Martha, who is always (t)here
my children Inbal, Eyal, and Ben, my beloved family group
and my group psychotherapy list members who became my
internal group

New International Library of Group Analysis Foreword

Since their inception the social sciences have been concerned with the effects of technology on the other components and dimensions of the social systems of societies, organisations, and other kinds of social grouping. Technology shapes the structures and processes of all social systems, and, in turn, is shaped by the other components of them. In fact, technology is often discussed in terms of a "socio-technical" system, in much the same way that the economy is discussed in terms of "political-economy". Technology also influences the psychology of the members of social systems; for example, through their modes of communication and their sense of control over their environments, and perhaps even with respect to their sense of what is "possible". Thus, we might consider the psychology or, to be more precise, the social psychology of technology. Clearly, technology can and should be studied from the point of view of group dynamics and perhaps group analysis in particular. This is especially apposite to information technology, ironically called "IT".

Various kinds of groups are often denoted in terms of their members being in face to face contact and communication with one another. Of course, "large groups" are even defined in terms of the number of people who cannot be in face to face contact with one another within a specific time and space. However, on the basis of modern information technology we have the possibility and indeed the actuality of so called "virtual groups", who are not actually confined by time and space, at least not in the usual way. Actually, virtual groups should be called "groupings", because in so far as their existence is totally dependent on their communication technology, they are a very special kind of group.

It is appropriate to refer to the technological unconscious and perhaps the technological non-conscious and pre-conscious of such groups as a particular dimension or even sub-category of their social unconscious in general (Hopper & Weinberg, 2011). The members of virtual groups are unaware of how extensively and intensively their lives, their relationships, and their personalities are restrained and constrained by their technology, not only in the world of work but also in other realms of their relations, including those in which they are most intimate. For example, historically the conduct of intimate relations has been augmented by letter, then by telephone, and more recently by devices that have gone beyond the simple medium of the telephone. It would seem that intimacy no longer requires the use of senses, such as touch and smell, which can be discussed in terms of the shift from a two person arrangement of classical psychoanalysis to a multi-person arrangement of group analysis in which there has been a shift from an analogy with the infant–mother relationship to the analogy of the collective mind of the family and other early groups of peers. The former arrangement is saturated with what a person can sense of another, but in the latter arrangement this information is highly diluted and even confused. Thus, a group analytical study of virtual groups is inevitably both an essay in the application of the group analytical perspective to the study of groups in general, and the study of the provision of therapy in groups.

The potential for therapeutic experience within virtual groups is great, and in the context of modern society and its contemporary modes of work and communication, very badly needed. Although this topic has begun to be explored with respect to telephone and video/Skype communications (Scharff, 2013), it has hardly been imagined with respect to group therapy in general, and certainly not to group analysis and psychoanalytical group psychotherapy.

However, during the last couple of years or so, I have often used IT technology for psychotherapeutic consultations and sessions, and I have experimented with Skype communications when members of groups have been unable to attend, because various emergencies have kept them away or they have been travelling. I have placed a laptop on a small table or an empty chair within the circle of chairs, and the group has tried to function as though the absent member were actually present, which has proved to be very useful, although not without its problems.

In this context, Haim Weinberg, PhD is eminently and uniquely qualified to introduce the group analytical study of virtual groups and to the socio-technical unconscious. Having first qualified in 1974 in Electrical Engineering at the Haifa Technicon, Israel, Dr Weinberg qualified in 1980 as a clinical psychologist at Haifa University. He later completed the first Training Course in Group Analysis in Israel, and in 2006 was awarded his PhD in psychology at Manchester Metropolitan University. In 2006 Dr Weinberg emigrated to Sacramento, California where he now works as a clinical psychologist, providing individual, couple, family, and group psychotherapy, as well as supervision and consultation. He teaches at the Wright Institute, Berkeley and at the Alliant International University, Sacramento. He is also a faculty member of the group facilitators training program in Tel-Aviv University. In addition he has developed a doctorate programme focused on group therapy with a significant distance learning component, under the auspices of the Professional School of Psychology in Sacramento, using many internet facilities ranging from Google groups to Skype to Zoom.

His professional interests are in the areas of multi cultural issues, conflict resolution, trauma groups, large groups, and the social unconscious. It is entirely understandable that he should have developed a particular interest in the study of large virtual groups and their dynamic matrices.

Dr Weinberg encourages us to think about many questions concerning technology and communication in virtual groups and the relationships within them. For example, what is the current meaning of the word "alone", when at the same time that we are alone we can also speak, hear, and see other people, and of course be heard and seen by them? Does this give us a false sense of security that we are also being understood? What is the meaning of sending a "selfie", which has now been added to the list of new words by the *Oxford University Dictionary*, to another person or even to a large number of other people, some of whom are in the role of bystanders of witnesses to the transactions? Is there a way in which we are even more vulnerable and more exposed in the context of this style of communication than we are when in face to face interactions in relationships? The development of inexpensive and widely available "smart-phones" has brought a new dimension to the erotic nature of masturbation: for example, fantasies are no longer augmented only by films and videos of strangers, but also by images of people who are known to us and with whom we are engaged. It is not difficult to understand why such patterns of communication are so addictive. In the same way that electricity made it possible to have light for twenty-four hours a day and therefore to be able to work constantly, without reference to the natural rhythms of the sun, and the moon, and the stars, controlled by nature, we can now be in instant, virtual communication with particular people, friends, colleagues, and even strangers all over the world, which raises yet further questions about delayed gratification, not to mention the need for time for thinking before speaking, which has traditionally been the basis for good and clear communication.

Virtual groups, defined in terms of the members of a communication network based on the use of IT, are certainly not the same as other kinds of groups who sometimes communicate through IT, such as committees or boards who meet face to face in a particular time and space, but who sometimes arrange "conference calls", or vice versa, and who at least know that they could meet if necessary. In fact, when it is difficult for such committees to meet face to face in a particular space on a regular basis, IT communication is likely to enhance the development of the relationships among the members, although presumably in ways that are different from what might happen if all communications took place face to face. I myself know how difficult it is to maintain a reasonable balance between involvement and detachment when caught up in the power of communication processes of virtual groups. I have found myself suddenly merging with the unconsciously imagined group, plunging into a role that is infused with projections. It is so easy to be caught up in projective and introjective processes which I would have thought would occur only in face to face communications.

I strongly recommend this lucid and accessible book to all those who are interested in the development of virtual groups. This book also serves as a good introduction to the study of group analysis as a way of understanding groups and how they function, but especially as a therapeutic modality. Although this monograph started its life as a PhD thesis, it has become a very readable text that has not suffered the loss of a depth of insight and scholarly balance.

Earl Hopper, PhD
Series Editor

Introduction

The title of this book is *The Paradox of Internet Groups*. What is this paradox that is so typical to virtual groups? Actually, there is more than one paradox: am I here, in my room, writing on my computer, or there, in Cyberspace, taking part in a group discussion? Am I detached, untouched, looking at the interactions from a distance and experiencing them as unreal, or touched, involved (perhaps even enmeshed), invested and experiencing the interaction as very real? Do I feel close, intimate, and interested in those people I have never met, or do I see them as strangers that do not really interest me, unlike people I meet face-to-face? Do I really care about these participants living thousands of miles from my place, or am I just curious about unknown cultures or have the urge to peep into other people's lives?

Internet groups are paradoxical because both sides of the above questions feel true. Not only can I be involved and uninvolved in Internet groups at different times, while still feeling that I belong and am part of those groups, I can also feel involved and uninvolved *at the same time*. I can feel my individuality, keeping my self-boundaries and deciding how much I want to self-disclose to the virtual forum, and at the same time sensing that I am part of a vast world-wide-web, immersed in a matrix of connections, feeling part of an encompassing environment. I am alone at my computer with no one else nearby, and still feel togetherness with other people who are far away, yet feel as close. They are not experienced as being far away because we all belong to this endless–boundless playground/playgroup transitional/intersubjective space. I can feel limited, perhaps deprived, not being able to see the faces of the people I communicate with or touch those with whom I developed close (online) relationship, and still feel that through these connections I can rise above the limitations of time and space. Throughout this book I will show that common dilemmas in human relationships, yielding only an either/or solution in face-to-face connections, find a "both" solution in virtual relationship and online forums.

This book is about groups on the Internet. It is not about Facebook, Twitter, YouTube, or other social networks. It is about Internet forums, discussion lists, and listserves. One might ask, why write a book about those discussion groups when social networks are flourishing? The answer is simple: I am not an expert in social networks. I am an expert in groups (especially therapy groups), and in my humble opinion I have developed an expertise in Internet groups. I also think that discussion lists and Internet forums are still attractive to millions of people, have different dynamics than social networks (perhaps because of the difference in privacy) and cannot be replaced by Facebook. Although millions of people take active roles (or an active role) in these Internet groups, experiencing feelings and dynamics very similar to "real" groups, the Internet groups remain understudied. It is important to unfold this phenomenon in order to explore further social networks dynamics as well.

I became involved with Internet communication at the beginning of the 1990s, when the Internet was still called Bitnet and served the academic exchange of ideas. Internet groups attracted my attention after a few years and in 1995, long before many people used the Internet for interaction, e-commerce and retrieval of information, I started my group psychotherapy discussion list. When I started this *listserve*, I never imagined where it would lead me. The Internet was quite young and my interest in group psychotherapy was growing. I missed learning about group work outside Israel, where I lived at that time, and thought it might be a good idea to use the new technology to open a forum where colleagues could discuss issues in their field of interest and learn from one another. I felt at ease with technology, unusual for a psychologist, due to my background as an electrical engineer. The result was quite surprising: within a few months, without a lot of advertising and by word of mouth, hundreds of people joined the forum, many of them writers of books and articles and quite well known in the field of group psychotherapy. In a short while we had more than 400 subscribers from thirty countries (although 75% were from the US). It seemed as if there was a real need for such a communication network.

As the volume of e-mails accumulated and discussions spread from professional issues to personal and interpersonal matters, I started feeling peculiar and surprised: the processes on the *listserve* reminded me of similar dynamics in my regular, face-to-face therapy groups. The level of cohesion that developed was unexpectedly high and resembled a small group, and the attitude of people toward me, the group manager (if this is the right term), reminded me of idealisation I encountered in some stages of my face-to-face groups. When I first came to the AGPA conference in New York in 1997, a year and a half after launching my group psychotherapy discussion list, I was received with admiration (which made me surprised and embarrassed) as an "Israeli genius" who developed an "original" means of communication for group therapists. It was clear to me that many projections were involved in this process. Little by little it dawned on me that the Internet forum is actually a group, some of its dynamics similar to those found in small therapy groups, some reminiscent of processes typical of a large group, and some related to unconscious aspects originating from the psychology of the Internet. While trying to find my way as the leader of this *listserve* group (or forum)—navigating among facilitating, conducting, and moderating the discussion—I started developing my understanding of these forums and the role of their conductor.

As said above, I have been managing my group psychotherapy forum since 1995. In the first years, once I understood how the forum resembles a group, I focused more on its similarity to a small group, writing about it (Weinberg, 2001) and conducting it accordingly. Later, I came to see how different an Internet forum is from a small face-to-face group, and I saw it more like a large group, albeit a large group in the darkness. More recently, features typical to Internet groups that are different from any face-to-face groups have become apparent and have forced me to develop a different approach to the role of the Internet forum conductor.

I still felt like an isolated pioneer. Then in 2002, following the publication of my first article about the forum dynamics, I was invited to a meeting of a group of Israeli mental health professionals, each of them the leader of an Internet forum. Many of them were leading open-to-the-public forums about psychological issues, while I was leading a discussion group for professionals, but it did not matter. It was amazing to see that we were dealing with similar difficulties; struggling to figure out the dynamics of the forums and how to moderate them. We established our own forum in order to exchange ideas about leading Internet groups. Apparently, their main difficulty has been with "trolls" (someone who posts inflammatory and extraneous messages in an online community). We creatively tried to use self-psychological interventions with these persons. Thinking about it today, I can see the similarity between these difficult-to-handle forum participants and what are called "difficult patients" in a group. For a few years, this forum of "managers of Internet forums" was my reference group. My main conclusion from these interactions is that leading an Internet forum requires special knowledge about the psychology of the Internet and the dynamics of its forums, as well as the psychological sensitivity, knowledge, and skills of a group therapist.

Who should read this book? In a way, everyone, as what is written in this book relates to modern circumstances. But perhaps different populations should approach this book wearing a different pair of glasses for different purposes. Psychotherapists who want to become updated might be interested in understanding the source of attraction of online groups for their patients. Those who are only used to face-to-face therapy might find it surprising that Internet connections have no less of an impact than interactions in "real" life. Group psychotherapists will find some similarities between the processes described in Internet forums and their face-to-face groups, expanding their understanding of group processes. Group analysts will enjoy the application of Foulkes and his followers' concepts to this new world of relationship. Students of group processes will certainly learn about universal and unique group dynamics described in this book. People who are involved in virtual groups would like to understand what is happening to them and their virtual friends online. And it is also, perhaps, for those who use the Internet daily and become curious about what makes them tick when they connect online. In short, this is *the* book for those interested in this specialised knowledge, whether they intend to lead Internet groups, are interested in groups in general or in group psychotherapy and group analysis in particular, or are just curious about the Internet and what is hidden in its vast spaces.

A previous version of some portions of this book was included in my PhD dissertation at the Manchester Metropolitan University (instructed by Erica Burman and Ian Parker), focusing on the culture of groups and the Internet unconscious, but most of the material is new.

In Chapter One, I introduce the main uses of the Internet, and the concerns about these uses. I highlight the universal human need to connect and argue that it is all about relationship. I also focus on the paradox of belonging and the constraints of relationship.

Chapter Two introduces the frame of reference of group analysis and how I use this theoretical perspective in this book as a qualitative research tool to explore processes in Internet groups. I suggest the existence of "image" neurons in addition to the well-known mirror neurons, associated with mirroring and empathy in face-to-face inter-actions, and discuss the lack of empathy on the Internet and the surprising caring in online group.

In Chapter Three I research culture as something ubiquitous, constructing our minds beyond our awareness, and its connection to groups. On the Internet, cultures of "me-ness" and "we-ness", result in what we can call "in-betweeness".

Chapter Four focuses on what it means to be present, especially online. The implications for groups and relationship online are considered.

Boundaries are the main issue of Chapter Five, as Cyberspace is a vast boundless space. I argue that the Internet's loose boundaries, creating a leaking container, require the presence of the group leader.

Chapter Six describes the dynamics of an Internet forum, trying to show both the similarities and differences between these dynamics and those occurring in a small group and a large group.

Chapter Seven focuses on the social unconscious, the possibility of an Internet unconscious and how they impact one another. I explore the idea of different kind of disembodied intimacy (which I term E-ntimacy©) developing online, and multi-culturalism on the Internet.

Written together with Ravit Raufman, Yalom's therapeutic factors and their existence in Internet groups are discussed in Chapter Eight.

In our opinion (supported by research), most of them, typical to small groups, can be found in online groups.

In summarising the main findings of research, final conclusions are explored and discussed, as well as directions for further research.

I hope you enjoy reading this book as much as I enjoyed writing it.

CHAPTER ONE

It is all about relationships

Internet popularity and its spread

In December 1995, sixteen million people around the world were using the Internet, accounting for 0.4% of the population in the world at that time. In June 2010, it was estimated that 1,966 millions of people were using the Internet, which equals 26.7% of the world's population (www.internetworldstats.com/stats.htm). This means that the use of the Internet multiplied itself by more than 123 times within fifteen years. It seems that the use of the Internet is accelerating and its impact on everyday life is enormous. In some continents, such as North America, the growth between 2000 and 2010 was 146%. In Africa this growth is estimated as 2,350%. Some of this impact is direct and clear, and some is subtle and covert.

A 2010 poll for the BBC World Service (news.bbc.co.uk/2/hi/8548190.stm) discovered that almost four in five people around the world believe that access to the internet is a fundamental right. The survey was conducted among more than 27,000 adults across twenty-six countries. Countries such as Finland and Estonia have already ruled that access is a human right for their citizens. In 2011 the United Nations also ruled that internet access is a human right (www.huffingtonpost.com/2011/06/08/internet-access-human-right-united-nations-report_n_872836.html).

Actually, we do not need this statistical evidence to become aware of how much the Internet has spread around the world and to be convinced of its importance in the life of people everywhere. We intuitively sense the impact of being connected online on our daily behaviour. What is more difficult to perceive and understand is the deeper, subtle and sometimes unconscious ways in which Cyberspace crawls into our minds.

The three areas of Internet use

Internet activity and use can be divided into three big arenas: information, transactions, and interactions.

Information is about data. When we use the Internet as a source of information, it actually serves as a huge database, from which we can retrieve the relevant information for our purposes. Whether we look at Google maps for directions, check the weather, read the news online, search Wikipedia to learn about Socrates, or even search for a scientific article on group therapy, we relate to the Internet as a hard drive which stores gigabytes of information. In this way, the Internet fulfils Asimov's vision of Multivac, the universal computer that accumulated every bit of information across generations (see en.wikipedia.org/wiki/Multivac).

The main difficulties with this use of the Internet are finding the relevant information, distinguishing between important data and inaccurate or insignificant ones, and not getting lost in the flood of information. The advantage of the Internet in this area is obvious: it saves us a lot of time and energy. Instead of going to the library and spending hours looking for an article, waiting for the newspaper to reach our door in order to read the news, or keeping maps of all the cities in the area, we can retrieve the data with a click of a mouse.

Transactions include commercial and business activity, also known as E-commerce. Many times this activity is formal and involves connecting with machines. Here are some examples: checking bank statements, paying a bill through PayPal, purchasing a flight ticket, or registering for a conference. This use of the Internet saves us time and energy as well. From the vendor's point of view the Internet poses a huge advantage. A small business in a forgotten town can reach hundreds of thousands of clients, something which they could have never dreamt of before the Internet. Big companies can save a lot of money by replacing human salespersons with automatic transactions, and bank personnel can be reduced because many services can be done online. However, as traditional business strategies are losing out to new, unconventional tactics, businesses must be flexible enough to survive in Cyberspace. In fact, more and more commercial transactions are executed this way, and it is estimated that in 2011 US E-commerce and online retail sales are projected to reach $197 billion, an increase of 12% over 2010 (http://en.wikipedia.org/wiki/Electronic_commerce).

The main problem in this kind of activity is confidentiality. Because our private financial information might be violated, we need to use passwords, protected websites, and other techniques to keep our privacy and prevent identity theft.

Interactions make up the field that interests us in this book. Writing e-mails to friends, communicating in Internet forums and listserves, posting on a website that is aimed at dating, using social networks such as Facebook, or even writing a blog or commenting to someone's blog, or to a posted video on YouTube: all these activities involve exchange of ideas, connecting with people, and focusing on relationship. Where other areas of using the Internet receive a balanced criticism of their pros and cons (most of the time looking at the benefits more than at the disadvantages), the various ways of connecting through the Internet have mostly encountered a negative attitude, not by avid users, whose numbers increase exponentially, but by scholars, writers, researchers, and journalists.

Criticism and concerns about using the Internet

We can find numerous articles criticising the Internet and the relationships that typify it. "Virtual relationship" they are titled, "shallow and unreal" people say, "nothing compared to face-to-face interaction". Authors wonder how we deteriorated from the art of writing letters that was so highly esteemed in the eighteenth century, to this quick-impulsive-one-sentence response of emails, or even worse, in text messages, where even the original words are abbreviated (u instead of you) to be more efficient. The criticism, as in the example above, is not limited only to Internet communication, but to all forms of electronic communication that became so popular in the twenty-first century. It usually comes from people who grew up in days where the world-wide-web (www) was only a fantasy in Asimov's science fiction stories (e.g., Multivac, the universe computer, as mentioned above). This critique is aimed toward young people who were born into a world where cell phones are taken for granted.

Here is an example from an article in the Washington Post published on 8 August 2010 (Shapira, 2010): "A generation of e-mailing, followed by an explosion in texting, has pushed the telephone conversation into serious decline, creating new tensions between baby boomers and millennials—those in their teens, 20s and early 30s". The writer even suggests a psychological explanation for the overuse of text messages by youngsters at the expense of phone calls: ". . .the immediacy of a phone call strips them of the control that they have over the arguably less-intimate pleasures of texting, e-mailing, Facebooking or tweeting."

Clearly, the difference in communications preferences has created a palpable perception gap between young adults and their parents. "What do you mean, you have 300 friends on Facebook?" I heard a father asking his son. "What is the meaning of friendship if you do not really know most of them? Will any of these "friends" come for your help when you need them, as true friendship should be?" Parents and people above their forties seem to forget that they had the same kind of misunderstandings with their parents while they were adolescents, although around other issues: "You are going steady," my father used to ask me, "and without knowing her parents or family? How is that possible?"

Some writers go as far as to say that Facebook has revolutionised the way we relate to one another more than anything since the invention of postal service. The question is whether this revolution positively changes relationships or has a deteriorating impact on the quality of relations. On the one hand we can point out that this way of connection through e-mails, Internet forums or online social networks such as Facebook, is the best adaptation to a fractured, dynamic world. It expanded the number of people we could meet every day from a handful to hundreds. It removed the time constraint from our social networking. Usually, in the face-to-face world, we invest a large amount of time to a limited number of friends (some estimate it as 40% of our limited social time devoted to five friends). On Cyberspace we can "talk" to as many people as we like. It is true that the amount of time invested in relationship determines the depth and quality, so probably many of these texted relations are not very deep.

In reality, research is not so consistent about the impact of Internet relationship on its users. Take, for example, a study by Kraut et al. (1998) that showed a correlation between Internet use and declines in social relationships and isolation. As you might expect, they found that greater use of the Internet was associated with small, but statistically significant declines in social involvement and with increases in loneliness as measured by communication with the family and the size of people's local social networks.

That paper was titled the "Internet paradox" because although the Internet is heavily used for communication, it makes people lonelier. Strong relationships developed online are rare, according to this study, and most people use the internet to keep up with offline relationships. So far it seems that this study suits the criticism and the expectations of many scholars who claim that more Internet use results in less human connectedness. But when Kraut et al. (2002) repeated their research four years later, they showed that the internet had a positive effect on social and psychological well-being. Unsurprisingly, this was more pronounced for extroverts and more socially connected people.

In fact, the latest conclusion about the impact of the Internet on relations (see October, 2013, http://suite101.com/a/internet-anti-social-behavior-theory-unfounded-a111897 and September, 2011, www.calsouthern.edu/content/srticles/technology-impact-on-social-relationships-surprising-data) is that, despite early studies suggesting that Internet use leads to anti-social behaviour, later findings indicate positive aspects of engaging in online socialising. Apparently, cyber or online social networking may increase a person's social ease, the breadth and depth of off-line relationships, and their overall "social capital"—the resources accumulated through the relationships with people.

Change of focus in public concerns about Internet risks

At the beginning of Internet era use and e-mail communication, psychologists believed that it would prove positive for socially phobic or shy people. They assumed that the anonymity typifying this kind of communication will help people with low self-esteem overcome their difficulties with connection. So when speculating about positive results, they usually restricted them to this problematic population. This point of view was clearly short-sighted and totally wrong. It is not the first time that psychologists have not been so good in predicting the outcome of a technological / social revolution.

Being a group psychotherapist, this false assumption—misunderstanding the nature of the beast and the potentially deep meaning of Internet communication—reminds me of the misconceptions about who is suitable for group therapy: that is, assuming that it is beneficial only for people with social phobia or lacking social skills, a premise still common among therapists who work only individually. This premise has nothing to do with the diversity of human problems that can be helped by the group.

On the other hand, when assessing the dangers of the net from the psychological point of view, there was and continues to be a lot of concern around creating false identities, becoming Internet addicted, and giving up social interaction in the real world. Notice how many negative implications these authors related to connecting over Cyberspace, concluding that pathologies developed will outgrow pathologies "cured". As an example, one of the work groups established for creating the new *DSM 5* explored substance related disorders and recommended that the diagnostic category include both substance use disorders and non-substance addictions and other addiction-like behavioural disorders such as "Internet addiction". They finally decided that such categories will be considered as potential additions to this diagnosis as and if data accumulates.

We can track the development and changes of fears around Internet use by observing and following the concerns of parents about their children's use of this "monster". In the historical development of the social concerns about the use of the Internet, we can identify two eras. In the first period, which lasted until around 2005, writers were worried more about Internet abuse (overuse of the Internet at the expense of other social activities). This period followed the excessive use of video games (see the popular science fiction movie "Tron", from 1982), and the danger seemed to be that children could drift into a dream world, play "Dungeons and Dragons" all day long, use the Internet to hide their real identity, thus learning to cheat and lie about their true self, or become confused about who they are.

In one of the important books about the psychology of the Internet written at that time, *Life On the Screen* (1995), Sherry Turkle, a sociologist and psychologist usually researching psychoanalysis and culture, did her best to convince the readers that there is no danger, and that the opposite is true. She claimed that assuming different personal identities in computer fantasy games may be therapeutic, because it is an opportunity to experience the multiple facets of the self (this idea about the multiple self was elaborated by relational psychoanalysts, such as Steven Mitchell and others). No other environment, she claimed, can provide such experimentation. What would be considered pathological in the "real" world (e.g., diffused identity disorder (DID) or psychopath) is perfectly normal in Cyberspace.

It is interesting to notice how the concerns about the Internet shifted around the middle of the first decade of the twenty-first century, perhaps along the massive use of Facebook (launched in 2004 and acquiring 800 million users in 2011). More and more fears were expressed about the "dark side" of Cyberspace, such as an easy access to pornography, being exploited by child perpetrators, and other safety concerns. If in the first half of the decade concerns were expressed more about hiding the true identity of the writers, and keeping personal information too private, thus creating an "illusion of truth" or a dream world in Cyberspace, in the second half, the opposite worry emerged: lack of privacy and being too exposed to others. Parents became worried that their children might meet someone dangerous through the Internet, give away personal information, and lose their privacy. As an example for the public concerns, on 9 November 2010 the New York Times published an article about an attempt to pass a law for a "do not track" feature that would let Internet users tell Websites to stop surreptitiously tracking their online habits and collecting clues about age, salary, health, location, and leisure activities (www.nytimes.com/2010/11/10/business/media/10privacy.html). In a CyberEthics website under the title "The invisible enemy" we can find the following sentence: "Social networking sites and the mIRC are the number one cause of losing anonymity and human deception." (mIRC stands for Internet Relay Chat) (www.cyberethics.info/cyethics1/index.php?option=com_content&view=article&id=160&Itemid=30&lang=en).

The truth is that the risks encountered by young people on the Internet are less significant than is often believed. This has been demonstrated by a project co-funded by the European Union and the London School of Economics and Political Science that surveyed more than 25,000 EU Kids of nine to sixteen year olds and their parents in twenty-five countries. The researchers (Livingstone, Haddon, Görzig, & Ólafsson, 2011) found that 93% of nine to sixteen year old users go online at least weekly. Fifty-nine per cent of them have a social networking profile and 26% report that their profile is public so that anyone can see it. However, being bullied online by receiving nasty or hurtful messages was found as relatively uncommon (6%), and it is quite rare for children to meet a new online contact offline (one in twelve children. Although for some parents 8% might still sound scary). Exposure to pornography is more common (although still only 14% report having seen images online that are obviously sexual). Interestingly enough, parents seem to be either unaware or deny that their children encounter these risks and around half of the parents whose children reported experiencing these risks did not realise it.

Most of the current criticism of the Internet relates to questions of privacy and warns us about possible violations of our privacy online. In fact, the global use of online communication, social networking and other Internet tools, challenges our commonly held assumptions about which information should be regarded as public and which should be viewed as private. Some experts within the field of Internet security and privacy express an extreme opinion that privacy does not exist; "Privacy is dead—get over it."

The question of privacy and keeping information confidential is very relevant to psychotherapists who see it as a fundamental rule in therapy, creating safety in the therapeutic relationship. Group therapists have a special interest in this question because in a group, it is not only the therapist who is bound to confidentiality, but every member of the group as well. In a way, trusting other members of the group to not make use of the information one reveals during the sessions and to keep it strictly confidential is based on quite a naïve mutual trust and more on an agreement to believe without testing whether participants' privacy is kept. Does this belief remind the reader of the way some people naively believe their privacy is kept on the Internet? In a later chapter (Chapter Five), we will more deeply explore these issues of boundaries, the public and private spheres, and how they are influenced by the Internet through the lens of group analysis.

The need to connect

In my opinion, many scholars and critics of the Internet miss an important question to be asked: if the Internet is perceived as so dangerous, what makes people use it so excessively? Assuming that people are aware of its risks—and it is difficult not to be aware when the dangers are stated in the media everyday (the number of websites warning about online risks and providing tips for safe use is enormous)—why do they still expose themselves to these dangers? We might assume that they are aware and taking the right measures to reduce the danger. Even if that is true, at least one possible meaning is that there must be something in Internet communication that answers the deep needs of many people.

Those who claim that Internet connections are shallow and virtual miss the important point: *it is all about relationships*. It does not matter whether we create deep relationships and how real they are. The crucial issue is that we desperately need to feel connected, to be in a relationship, to feel that we belong, and that we are part of a community, or perhaps even part of something bigger than ourselves, and the Internet provides an illusion of being connected to the world with the tip of your finger. When it comes to connectivity, support systems, and a sense of belonging, no other tool can provide these needs so quickly and easily.

The need to connect is very human, starting from infancy and never ending. Attachment theory claims that from birth we are attached to our care-givers and need this emotional bonding. The same motivational system is responsible for the bond that develops between adults in emotionally intimate relationships. Recent research in neurobiology found out that we are wired for social relationships. Cozolino (2006) shows how our brains are structured and function as highly social organisms. He illustrates how the architecture and development of brain systems from before birth through adulthood determine how we interact with others. The human brain and nervous system are built and sculpted, neuron by neuron, through the interaction of our particular genes and relational experiences. The last decades, beginning with the discovery of mirror neurons in 1992, initiated a proliferation of research in neurosciences, changing our assumptions about human nature. We have moved from *Homo homini lupus* (man is a wolf to man), and the focus on aggression and competition in psychology, to a view of the social brain with emphasis on cooperation and altruistic behaviour in human systems. Instead of talking about "the selfish gene" scientists and scholars talk about "the altruistic gene" and, instead of emphasising the parts of the brain involved in aggressive behaviour, we emphasise now the empathic parts.

It is a truism that life in modern society is reported to be more and more alienated and disconnected. The emphasis on money and materialistic goods in Western countries, the fragmentation of the family in many societies, living in big crowded cities, frequent relocation due to work pressures, and many other sources, including the diminution of communitarian values in mobile cultures, contribute to the loss of social support systems and feelings of isolation. As interconnected humans who frequently feel a deep disconnect, we need community desperately.

Encounter and sensitivity training groups in the US in the 1970s, based on a humanistic psychological theory and emphasising present experience, connection and human fulfilment, flourished as a response to an alienated society and lack of authentic human connections. They were based on the premise that individuals can be helped to make positive changes to their own attitudes and relationships and connect meaningfully with one another. In a society prioritising individuality and materialistic/financial achievements at the expense of human relationship, these groups attracted many people hungry for connection. Their impact went beyond the number of people going to Esalen (the famous centre for these groups) or participating in these groups, to become a cultural phenomenon of that time (reflected in movies such as *Bob and Carol and Ted and Alice*, 1969). We can find traces of the premises behind these groups in the focus on the here-and-now in most therapy groups and the idea of immediacy in the modern group analytic approach.

Connection over the Internet is the new answer to human isolation and alienation in modern society, and indeed a good answer for the need to be in relationship. It makes it easy to feel connected either to friends in other places (through e-mails or social networks), or to a community of people with the same field of interest (through listserves, forums, or professional networks). The quick (sometimes almost immediate) responses to requests or greetings from people beyond the oceans collapse time and space and create the illusion of immediacy. The ability to stay in touch with people we left behind when we relocated softens the feelings of loss. In a world typified by immigration and population mobility, the Internet suggests a solution to reduce psychological difficulties associated with such moves. As mentioned before, the feeling while writing and connecting on the Internet is that the world is at the tips of your fingers, thus replacing alienation with an exaggerated (sometimes even omnipotent) sense of taking part in the world.

An attractive, wide-spread, and successful technology should set its goal in attempting to replace a natural world that is indifferent to our wishes, with a world that is responsive to our wishes. The technology should be felt as a mere extension of the self. We need our tools to collaborate with us and restore the illusion of control that nature inherently makes impossible. That is why when our computers crash, sometimes we feel a slight depression. The Internet is successful in transforming a world of hurricanes and hardships, losses and broken hearts, into a world of support and connection. It is also successful in transforming a world of disconnection and isolation into a world of belonging. That does not mean that we do not encounter difficulties in relationship in Cyberspace. On the contrary, we can misunderstand many messages and project our inner world on the written text. We can face flame wars and "trolls" in Internet forums. But we still feel that we can control the communication much more than in a face-to-face interaction: at least we can turn off the computer and go to bed . . .

Relationship and its constraints

Every relationship takes away some degree of freedom from the people involved. This range of loss of freedom extends from sometimes having to spend time with casual friends when you wish to be somewhere else, all the way through to the norm of having monogamous sex with only one partner in loving relationship. As we know, some people have difficulty staying in long-term relationships. The commitment required for being in such a relationship is too much for them, and fear of losing themselves or their freedom overcomes their need for connection. Other people shy away from any formal belonging to organisations, associations or even societies because they are worried that this commitment will "enslave" them to the extent that they will not feel free to do what they want. Indeed, belonging to any formal group usually means obeying its rules and collaborating with its norms. This is a common dilemma in human relationship, and up to a certain extent, quite a normal one.

In fact, this is one of the focal conflicts we can expect at the beginning of any therapy group, as MacKenzie and Livesley (1983) stated in their model of group development. The question every member faces at that stage is whether to take part, belong and feel involved in the group or stay outside and feel isolated and disconnected. Each group members resolves this dilemma in their own way, reflecting how they deal with this issue outside the group.

The real question is not whether you lose your independence but to what extent you give up some freedom and what you gain in return. One of the common mistakes is to define the dilemma as an "either/or" issue, an "all or none" question. This mistake is based on a rigid (maybe immature) definition of freedom as the absence of any obligations, responsibilities, and duties. According to this definition, freedom is doing whatever I want at any time, disregarding any consequences. This premise leads to the conclusion summarised in the slogan: "to be free is to be totally alone". A more mature and balanced view about relationship takes into consideration the point of view of the other partner (an intersubjective approach), understanding that commitment ensures safety: that, surprisingly, when the other person is ready to give up some freedom and commits, you feel more freedom due to the secure attachment. The same point of view can be adopted for organisations and societies: rules and norms create a safety net and help the member of the group feel protected. People who are too focused on the fear of losing their independence or freedom in close relationship usually forget what they gain in this arrangement.

The Internet allows for less committed relationships. In fact, it allows for an illusion of control over the amount of commitment people want to develop in any connection. The fact that we cannot see a face on the screen when we communicate with the other (unless we use video conversation), always involves more projections and more problems with boundaries. On the downside it can lead to dehumanisation and depersonalisation of the other, and to phenomena such as bullying, flaming, and insensitivity. On the positive side it might help us to feel less guilty and less obliged to relationship that is not really deep, thus allowing for a healthy deviation from or defiance of false social norms. As much as it sounds strange and paradoxical, social norms about the "right" behaviour in daily uncommitted relationships can be quite maladaptive in the deep sense and in the long run. Although on the surface it helps creating a nice atmosphere when people greet me with "How are you?" at the supermarket, in fact it is a superficial question, void of meaning, stated only out of conformity with social consensus. In the long run, the polite-nice mask we wear as part of our social persona is glued to our face, creating a partly false self. Internet communication frees us from the necessity to always wear this mask, and this is part of its charm.

The same sense of freedom applies to the issue of belonging to groups, associations, or communities. We expect members to keep a steady continuous involvement with the groups they belong to. A member of a church, who comes to service every Sunday and then disappears for a month with no explanation, will arouse either concern or irritation among other members. This is very true for therapy groups as well, and people who do not obey this rule of continuous presence (many times specifically requested in the group agreement) are pressured to return to the norm by other group members as they disturb the sense of stability and safety. In Internet forums, listserves, and communities, this pressure to continuously attend the meetings is gone. Of course, there are no "meetings", and the member can come and go, read and write, whenever s/he feels like doing so. The amount of involvement in Internet forums changes for many people throughout time. People who post regularly in Internet forums, and are pre-occupied with life troubles at some point, might temporarily withdraw from writing to the forum. However, they still feel like they are a part of the group, and will still be welcomed warmly when they return to posting. Again, control over the amount of involvement is not only possible, but also much more accepted and expected. In fact, as we will see when we discuss the dynamics of Internet groups, this is one of the aspects that distinguishes face-to-face groups from Internet groups. The ebb and flow of involvement in an Internet forum is a normal part of its existence. People who post regularly for some time might become lurkers (an Internet expression meaning being only a passive observing participant) sometimes, *and get back to being more active* in the forum later with no problem. Their temporary disappearance is not such a source of disturbance to the group as in face-to-face or therapy groups.

Groups on the Internet reflect the conflict between the need to experience oneself as an autonomous agent who is masterful and in control versus the need to surrender (Ghent, 1999). Western culture focuses on becoming increasingly individuated, and promotes values as autonomy, independence, differentiation-individuation, personal agency, and responsibility. While these are important values (although heavily culturally biased), it is important not to lose sight of the costs associated with them: isolation, lack of meaning, alienation, and the experience of emptiness, or to lose sight of the need we all have to surrender—to have the experience that it is not all up to us, and that there is some benevolent force outside of us that we can trust and to which we can abandon ourselves: a sense that we are connected to others and to the cosmos. Participating and being involved in Internet forums and Cybercommunities definitely helps individuals feel this connection to others and to the universe.

A short note about the issue of boundaries in relations and the sense of self in connection to the question of freedom and commitment, a process to which we will return later when we talk about group and Internet boundaries. We all need some boundaries around ourselves (from physical, skin boundaries to psychological, territorial ones) in order to feel our individuality and differentiation, especially when we enter relationships. As in any living system, these boundaries are most useful when dynamic and fluctuate around a range that is not too rigid while still not too loose. Blurred boundaries in relationship lead to loss of a person's self and freedom while too rigid boundaries lead to lack of touch, isolation, and no flow of communication and energy between the relationship partners. Many people have some difficulty regulating and controlling boundaries well enough, not necessarily up to a pathological degree as we find in a borderline personality disorder. The Internet provides easier and more control of boundary regulation: We can disconnect from relationships that feel more threatening to our boundaries and sense of self, simply by ignoring e-mails and messages. We can get back to these interactions after we worked through (consciously or unconsciously) our internal boundaries and restored our balance, thus regulating flexible boundaries.

Summary and conclusion

Internet connections and communication have drawn a lot of criticism from scholars, researchers, and parents, ranging from fears of losing one's identity, creating false selves, and becoming addicted. At the beginning of Internet commentary, there was often an expressed devaluing of any relationships developed on Cyberspace, seeing them as shallow and unreal, and fearing the loss of privacy. In fact, many of these fears are unjustified, but more than that—they do not capture the true essence and charm of Internet connections. Actually, it is all about relationship, and the Internet is *the* current solution to the needs of people to connect and belong. In our modern world typified by immigration, relocation, alienation, and isolation, the Internet provides the perfect answer to these problems.

Add to the above the fact that Internet connections allow for a healthy regulation of commitment and involvement with the other and with groups, more than in face-to-face relationship, and you might start understanding that there is also some blessing in this new way of interacting with people.

CHAPTER TWO

The frame of reference of group analysis

The unique frame of reference that I use in this book to understand groups on the Internet is the group analytic one. Group analysis (Foulkes, 1975) is much more than a therapeutic approach and is grounded in the social sciences. It is a way of analysing data and looking at the world: it is a research tool. Group analysis is as much a methodological system as a theoretical system (Parker, 1997). It is useful for the analysis of small therapeutic group processes but also for the analysis of large groups such as communities, ethnic groups, and even societies. It provides tools to analyse unconscious processes and learn about society and communities (including Internet communities) in more depth. In this chapter I will describe how group analysis illuminates the philosophical, sociological and psychological aspects of groups, cultures and society at large.

Group analysis as a qualitative research tool

In the previous century research has been dominated by the scientific method. This positivist and quantitative research emphasised objectivity, neutrality, measurement, and validity. In the last forty years the domination of positivism has been challenged. Increased dissatisfaction with its primary position has led to the development of a variety of methodologies (Lather, 1991). One of them is the qualitative research.

Qualitative research can be characterised as the attempt to obtain an in-depth understanding of the meanings and "definitions of the situation" presented by informants, rather than the production of a quantitative "measurement" of their characteristics or behaviour (Wainwright, 1997). Qualitative data sources include observation and participant observation (fieldwork), interviews and questionnaires, documents and texts, and the researcher's impressions and reactions. In this book, my data is the verbatim of the e-mail exchange in Internet forums. The decision regarding which vignettes to choose in order to demonstrate my observations is framed by the group analytic theory that guided my research.

Hunt (1989) drew our attention to the role of subjectivity in research. For Hunt, the research process is "hermeneutic"—an interpretative activity that aims for deeper understanding of the research material. For years, psychoanalysis has been considered too "subjective" for an objective examination. The emergence of qualitative research put psychoanalytic ideas back on the agenda, and enhanced its use as a research tool. The role of subjectivity in psychoanalytic research is crucial. Subjectivity is viewed by psychoanalysis, as with much qualitative research, not as a problem but as a resource (and topic). To draw upon one's own subjectivity in the research process does not mean that one is not being "objective" but that one actually comes closer to a truer account (Parker, 1997). Interestingly enough, the return of subjectivity to psychoanalytic research paralleled the emergence of the intersubjective approach in psychoanalysis (Benjamin, 1998; Mitchell, 1993), which emphasises the stance of the psychoanalyst not as an objective observer who seeks the truth but as a subjective participant in the therapeutic interaction.

But classical psychoanalysis as a research tool has its shortcomings too. It postulates a number of assumptions about the nature of human experience (such as "the unconscious", "the Oedipus complex", and "defences") and regards them as absolute truths. What is more important: psychoanalysis looks for the source of human problems within the individual, thus serving a hidden political agenda. Describing social problems as stemming from intra-psychic drives helps maintain the socio-political status quo, promising the continuation of cultural dominant forces (Prilleltensky, 1989). It means that change comes out of personal introspection and decision-making, and its stimulus is not a social one.

The relationship between the processes taking place inside the self and the social, cultural, and political processes happening outside the individual, but nonetheless affecting her/him, is one of the essential dilemmas for modern psychotherapy (Guigon, 1993). If the source of psychological problems lies within the individual and not his or her culture—then society and its political institutions can be left alone. If the source of problems is the individual, then it is s/he who needs therapy. This approach serves the social order and preserves it. Thus, therapy advances the interests of the socio-political elites. It might even be that psychotherapy perpetuates the same problems it offers as their solution (Sarason, 1985).

Group analysis, as we will see later, followed another direction: interpersonal, group, system, and social oriented. Thus it avoids the pitfalls of psychoanalysis that is looking only for interpsychic causes for distress. The ideas of "the-group-as-a-whole" (Ettin, Cohen, & Fidler, 1997), and understanding the voice of the individual as the voice of the group, shifts the focus from the one to the many, and from the individual to the organisation and society. The notion that the individual is inseparable from his/her culture points to the direction of change as brought by observing and analysing the mutual influences (all these ideas will be elaborated and explained in more detail later). Change is achieved by creating a holding environment and analysing, understanding and becoming aware of the processes in the group and in society.

The research paradigm shift from quantitative to qualitative methods mentioned earlier is only part of a larger paradigmatic shift taking place in the Western World in the late twentieth century. The move is manifested in many areas: from modernity to post-modernity, from nationalism to globalisation, from cultural supremacy of one group over others to the concept of multiculturalism and the acknowledgment of cultural diversity. As we shall see later, group analysis deals with social phenomena and processes, incorporating them with the subjective experience. Thus it is a very appropriate instrument for researching issues related to these social changes. Indeed, it is a suitable tool to research Cyberspace and to understand group phenomena over the Internet.

From the individual in the group to group analysis

The development of group psychotherapy in general and group analysis in particular is strongly related to other developments in the social and natural sciences, including general system theory (GST) as introduced into the scientific field by the biologist Von Bertalanffy after the Second World War. The mechanistic approach alone was no longer enough to understand complex systems. According to Von Bertalanffy (1956) GST deals with formulating and deriving the principles valid for every system in general. A system is defined as a set of elements in interaction. Although GST started with biological systems, it quickly expanded to other scientific areas, including behavioural, social and psychological ones (Buckley, 1967). Community psychiatric approaches, family therapy, and group therapy resulted from this development (Hill, 1972). Some assumptions of GST are especially attractive for analyses of human beings and groups. Although various systems exhibit a wide variety of behaviours, fundamentally they all possess a common underlying structure. Change takes place across system or sub-system boundaries. The idea that the particle is part of a bigger whole, and cannot be analysed outside its system, led to the notion that the individual cannot be studied out of the context with which we are dealing, whether it is the family, the group or society.

Pines (1981) characterises the evolution of group analysis as follows:

> The emergence of analytic group psychotherapy as a theory and as a technique was facilitated by a new scientific paradigm, that of the move from the study of the single entity, the item, the individual, to the study of the relationship between an entity and the field of forces in which other entities are encountered . . ... The classical psychoanalytic model of mental apparatus will not do, as it is based on one-body psychology. In group psychotherapy we need other models; perhaps a systems model will do. (page 276)

Adopting a system model for groups transforms group therapy from "the analysis of individuals in groups" to "group analysis". The paradigm is not that of psychoanalysing the member in the group setting, because the group is more than a background and the analysis is of that gestalt too. The idea of the group developing in stages

(MacKenzie, & Livesley, 1983; Tuckman, 1965), concepts such as "the group-as-a-whole" (Ettin, Cohen, & Fidler, 1997), the "mother group" (Foguel, 1994; Scheidlinger, 1974), and the emergence of the large group as an instrument for studying social systems (Schneider & Weinberg, 2003) could not become manifest without the broader understanding of groups as living systems.

Pines' description of group analysis cited above, reminds us of the updated relational approach in psychoanalysis. "The relational approach uses the concept of the relational matrix, the web of the relations between the self and other, as the overarching framework within which to house all sorts of psychoanalytic concepts" (Aron, 1996, p. 33). This means that the focus of therapy is on the relations between the therapist and the patient, and how each of them contributes to the evolving therapeutic relationship. It means moving from the "one-person psychology", where the therapist was interested in the patient's projections, transference, and resistance, to a "two-person psychology" (in individual therapy) where all these classical concepts acquire a different meaning.

Foulkes can be perceived as pioneer of relational approaches. Long before the distinction between one-person and two-person psychology emerged in articles, he defined group analysis as: "the analysis by the group, of the group, including its conductor" (Foulkes, 1975, p. 3). The inclusion of the conductor (the group analyst, in the Foulkesian terms) in the analysis brings in the notion that the group therapist's behaviours, thoughts, and feelings are part of the group process. This statement was Foulkes' way of saying that the therapist is not only the therapist "of" the group, but also "in" the group, that is, a therapist/ quasi-group member.

It is interesting that both Bion and Foulkes, the two pioneers of group psychotherapy in Britain, developed the notion of the group-as-a-whole at the same time, even though they never worked together and their theories are quite diverse. These ideas followed the tradition of the German Gestalt psychology arguing that the whole is not just the sum of its parts. One step further led them to argue that the group is more than the sum of its individuals and to the revolutionary idea (at that time) that the group defines its members and not vice versa. On the other side of the ocean, in the US, Trigant Burrow made a similar shift from psychoanalysis to working with groups, developing a pioneering thinking about the original nature of man as social

(Hinshelwood, 1999), and coined the term "group analysis" which Foulkes used later in his writings.

Group analysis understands the behaviour of the individual in terms of the whole group, just as social psychology understands the individual's behaviour in terms of the whole social group of which she/he is a member (Mead, 1968). Actually, the idea of changing the behaviour of the individual through the group is connected to the notion that deviant behaviour is created in the context of the social and family group. If we want to correct this malfunctioning, we need to get back to the original environment, a group environment. Foulkes's (1975) concept of "ego training in action" means that the individual's understanding of him/herself is promoted through the analysis of transference in communicative action in the group. It means "self development through subjective interaction" (Brown, 1994, p. 98) in the transitional space of the group. There is still the danger that the problematic behaviour in question will only repeat itself in the group, without being corrected. Foulkes (1948) had an answer for this possibility. He believed that group members reinforce each other's normal behaviour and correct their neurotic reactions. He shows a deep trust in the beneficial nature of the group, which in later years came to be highly criticised (Nitsun, 1996).

From group analysis to the analysis of social processes

Foulkes was interested and enormously influenced by the sociology of Norbert Elias (1978). Elias placed central importance on social relatedness, explored the political, philosophical, and psychological forces behind the dichotomy between the individual and the group and even inquired how these forces are institutionalised within the individual's psyche. Pines (2002) wrote that, according to Elias, the evolution of society profoundly affects individual psychodynamics. Summarising Elias's approach, he noted that as individuals civilise their behaviour and restrain their impulses, the strength of the social forces inside the individual increases; and the structure of the psyche changes. The civilising process described by Elias concerns libidinal energy in particular, invested in such activity as the management of eating, disposal of waste, cleanliness, and, of course, aggression. Society gradually monopolises the sanctioned use of violence, and self-restraint is rewarded by the protection of the law. Pines sees Elias's influence on group analysis in the psychoanalytic primacy of projection over introjection.

Elias wrote, "Humans . . . are made by nature for culture and society" (1991, p. 84). Following Elias, Foulkes wrote of, "The microcosm of the individual repeating and reflecting the microscopical changes of the society, of which he forms a part" (Foulkes, 1948, p. 14). So Foulkes sees the individual as embedded in and produced through the social. The theoretical and clinical infrastructure of group analysis was based on the central role of society and culture in the founding of the individual subject: The focus moved from the subject to culture. We will follow this shift by later focusing on culture and exploring the emergence of Internet culture through group analytic lens.

Foulkes shaped his ideas during his service as a psychiatrist in the Second World War in Northfield, an army base in the Midlands, England. There, he treated, together with several other colleagues, soldiers who suffered from the horrors of the war. The Northfield Experiment, as it became known, became a turning point for group psychotherapy, and most of the writers that influenced the British thinking about groups (such as Bion and Ezriel) developed their ideas there. Foulkes wrote his *Introduction to Group-Analytic Psychotherapy* (1948) following this experience. It is interesting to note that already in 1948 he related to group analysis in two different ways: as a new kind of treatment on one hand, to which he provided detailed instructions for the conductor's contributions, but also as a new psychological frame of reference relating to the individual only as an abstraction of social relations.

The basic position of group analysis is that through the group and the evolving interrelations of its members, the patient first reveals and ultimately heals or treats his or her individual subjectivity. Looking at it from this end, group analysis is used as a method of psychotherapy and deals with transference, counter-transference, defence mechanisms, and other practical matters developed to make this therapy more effective. A fine example of this approach to group analysis can be found in Foulkes's book *Group Analytic Psychotherapy, Method and Principles* (1975). But even when dealing with the practice of group analysis the deeply social nature of the human being is always there.

Group analytic concepts start from the individual and permeate to society (and also vice versa). The same group analytic terms are used in relation to the individual, the group and society at large. This is no surprise, because according to group analysis the individual is "penetrated" within a longitudinal network of trans-personal processes. Group analysis enables us to perceive the resonance among the social, interpersonal, and the intrapsychic levels of experience. So, within a group analytic frame we can see the importance of addressing the wider context beyond the personal.

Throughout this period, the development of the group analytic theory became more and more engaged with the analysis of social issues. Papers on gender, economy, culture, social regression, the impact of war, terror, and trauma, and the influence of the Internet have appeared lately in the *Group Analysis* Journal. Special issues of the journal were published about group analysis in the new millennium, relational goods and the social unconscious (detailed later). Small wonder that one of the most important books in group analysis, describing the developments of this theory towards the end of the previous century, is titled *The Psyche and the Social World* (Brown & Zinkin, 1994).

From the small group to the large group

Group analysts are interested in large groups no less than in small groups. Small groups are suitable for therapeutic purpose. They provide safe boundaries and perfect conditions for the development of trust, self-disclosure and therapeutic exploration. Traditionally, group psychotherapists work in small groups (a small group means seven plus or minus two), and focus on the here-and-now, avoiding the social and political events outside the group. When they deal with the social context they use the social and political events to explore what they mean for group members.

We can infer from processes in small groups to the wider environment, as the group is always a microcosm. But small groups typically develop a culture of their own that might be quite different from the culture outside them. In the previously mentioned atmosphere of safety that is created in the small group, intimacy develops and self-disclosure is possible. This is in a sharp contrast from the alienated environment we often encounter in our everyday life (and sometimes the source of attraction for those groups). In order to learn about bigger organisations, associations, and institutes, or even about culture, group analysts study psychological constellations that better simulate reality. They study human behaviour and group dynamics of a larger group (Kreeger, 1975). Large groups (from twenty and upward according to de Maré (1975), to forty to eighty according to Turquet (1975), and hundreds or even more, according to Volkan (2001)) allow the exploration of hidden dimensions, which do not appear in small group settings (Weinberg & Schneider, 2003).

The Association of Therapeutic Communities spread the culture of large groups by using them extensively in the psychiatric wards and hospitals of the 1970s. At the same time it flourished in the Group Analysis Symposiums and other group therapy conferences and organisations, also crossing the ocean to the US (Pines, 2003). Large groups provide opportunities for understanding powerful social constraints relating to authority, organisational dynamics, major-ity–minority group relations and other social conflicts. They can be used to explore the crystallisation of identities by looking at factors such as gender, political, religious, ethnic identities, and differences. Participating in a large group in a conference brings forth questions about the meaning of belonging to society and being a citizen. "Should I open my mouth?" "How much impact can my words have in this crowd?" "Wouldn't it be wiser not to enter this conflict?" are some of the questions typically crossing the participant's mind (Turquet, 1975; Weinberg & Schneider, 2003).

The large group is usually not the best forum for dealing with the specific feelings and pains of the individual and, often times can inten-sify feelings of aloneness. It cannot function as a form or type of psychotherapy, although, in some participants, there can be engen-dered feelings of containment. The large group is, however, an impor-tant tool in understanding social interactive processes and interrelationships within society. As de Maré writes: "The large group ... offers us a context and a possible tool for exploring the interface between the polarised and split areas of psychotherapy and socio-therapy. This is the area of the inter-group and of the transdisciplinary ..." (1975, p. 146).

The lesson we learn from unstructured large groups conducted in group therapy conferences is quite gloomy. On the dark side of relating to authority we can sometimes see infantile yearning for strong authority, leading to readiness of giving up one's judgment. Or unreasonable attack on authority out of what seems to be a regressive oedipal competition. The dynamic processes, and especially projections, projective-identifications, and splitting, might lead to stormy conflicts between subgroups and the emergence of crude aggression. The fear of losing oneself in the crowd (Freud, 1921c; Turquet, 1975), the threat of annihilation and alienation force the individual to use a variety of techniques to protect him- or herself, including clinging to familiar others, creating national, gender, religious, and other socio-political divisions, etc.

On the bright side we can explore the ways to avoid these dangers, from increasing awareness through interpretations and introspection to structuring the group or emergence of natural positive leaders. De Maré (1975), one of the pioneers of large and median groups, pointed out that while the function of the small group is to socialise the individual, the function of the large group is to humanise society.

The psychological processes in the large group are intensive and, by the use of the parallel process concept, we can understand them as representing what is happening in the outside world. The concept of parallel process has its origin in the psychoanalytic concepts of transference and countertransference. Processes in the large group replicate social and political processes. One of the merits of the large group is that we can use it to study the social unconscious.

We will see later that Internet forums and groups are actually a kind of large group disguised as a small group. Many typical processes and dynamics occurring in large groups can be seen in interactions typical for online groups. For example, expressions of alienation, aggression, being lost in the crowd, and losing one's voice appear on the Internet as well as in large groups (Weinberg, 2003b).

From the individual unconscious to the social unconscious

According to Freud's topographical model of personality organisation, psychic life can be represented in three levels of consciousness: the conscious, the preconscious, and the unconscious. Freud was not the first to talk about the unconscious. Already in 1765 Leibniz stressed that there are more perceptions apart from those of which the mind is aware. There are endless other perceptions that are not salient enough to be registered in the memory but can be recognised through their results. Many eighteenth and nineteenth-century philosophers agreed that we could not understand human behaviour without assuming an active, unconscious mental life. Freud added another dimension by stating that the unconscious is a mental apparatus with a different mode of functioning than the conscious one. Different rules conduct and govern the two systems: reality testing, rational thinking, and logical codes are typical of the conscious system but are absent from the unconscious one. Freud believed that significant aspects of human behaviour are shaped and directed by these unconscious irrational forces and that they are inadmissible to direct awareness. We can learn about the individual unconscious through the interpretation of fantasies, dreams, and slip of the tongue phenomena.

When we move to groups and see them as entities, a new kind of unconscious emerges: the group unconscious. Bion (1959) spoke explicitly of group mind and introduced concepts such as protomental system, basic assumption, and work group. Bion's basic assumptions (discussed later in this chapter) are examples of the group unconscious: nobody owns them and nobody wants to be responsible for them. Foulkes (1964) created the group matrix model to describe better that multidimensionality he thought to be characteristic of group thinking and communication. With the concept of "matrix", chosen for its clear link with the concept of *mater*, Foulkes aimed to underline the original and specific quality of group situation, not only depending on the sum of single members' personality features. The matrix shows its own structure and functional autonomy, in some way transcending individuals, even if it is constructed and shared by the whole of individuals. In fact the matrix is to some extent able to affect their thought, language, and behaviour. "In this sense we can postulate the existence of a group 'mind' in the same way as we postulate the existence of an individual mind" (Foulkes, 1964, p. 118). It is a product of the interaction of individual group members but is not static. Whether we term it the group mind, matrix, or unconscious it is clear that we are talking about some abstraction that is beyond the individual members of the group and not the simple adding of their individual minds. Like the individual unconscious we can only deduce about its existence from the group's acts or discourse.

The idea of the group unconscious and the hidden ways that groups affect their members is difficult to perceive by lay-people in the Western world, whose culture is based on the belief in free will and the individual right for the pursuit of happiness. Still there is a long-standing research tradition in social psychology showing the impact of the group on its members and their unawareness to this hidden exertion of power. Coming to the next level of abstraction is even more difficult to accept: the social unconscious. In general the idea of the social unconscious implies that we are driven by social forces of which we are unaware. These forces structure our behaviours, thoughts, and perceptions. This concept is different from the Jungian concept of the collective unconscious (Jung, 1934) because it represents unconscious dynamics that are specific to a certain society or culture, while the collective unconscious is universal, shared by all societies and based on the same hidden archetypes common to all human beings no matter to which society they belong.

The idea of the social unconscious construct is double-sided. On one hand it reflects social and cultural arrangements of which individuals are unaware (Hopper, 1996) and on the other, it means the representation of social forces and power relations in the psyche (Dalal, 2001). We can observe the social unconscious by resorting to a kind of binocular vision, where through one lens we focus on the restrictions, constraints, and limitations residing in the unconscious of people due to their belonging to society, and on the other, on the myths, anxieties, defences, and collective memories co-constructed by members of a specific society. Special consideration should be given to the study of the social unconscious in groups, especially large groups. The idea of the social unconscious assumes that some specific hidden assumptions guide the behaviour of a certain society or culture. In the same manner that unconscious forces drive an individual without him/her knowing it, a group, an organisation or the entire society can find itself acting upon unconscious forces too.

The term social unconscious was first mentioned by Foulkes in his book *Therapeutic Group Analysis* (1964): ". . . the group-analytic situation, while dealing with the unconscious in the Freudian sense, brings into operation and perspective a totally different area of which the individual is equally unaware. . . . One might speak of a social or interpersonal unconscious" (p. 52). It seems that Foulkes did his best to go beyond the classical Freudian concept of the individual unconscious to include the social and communicational forces affecting interpersonal and transpersonal processes. Hopper (1996, 2003) has contributed many papers to this concept, being one of the most consistent proponents of the social unconscious. He defines it as: "the concept of the social unconscious refers to the existence and constraints of social, cultural and communicational arrangements of which the people are unaware" (Hopper, 2001, p. 10). This definition means that living in a specific culture and belonging to a certain society has its influence on the behaviour of its members and their ways of communication without their noticing it. Observing from the outside, we can identify common behaviours and attitudes of people from the same society and culture. However, to people living in that society these aspects may be elusive and less obvious. Lately, Hopper and Weinberg (2011) published the first volume in a series of books about the social unconscious.

The Internet provides us with several ways to explore the social unconscious, both by researching the ways in which people from different cultures interact, (thus seeing how their social unconscious is reflected on the Internet), and analysing it. We can also ask ourselves whether there are some hidden assumptions about Cyberspace, creating what Weinberg (2003b) called the "Internet unconscious" and describe the unique elements that compose this intercultural, international web of relationship. There is yet another way of connecting between the Internet and the social unconscious. We can explore the ways in which the existence of the World Wide Web, and its widespread use almost from its inception, influenced our society, both consciously and unconsciously. A chapter about the Internet unconscious is included in this book (Chapter Seven).

From conservative group analysis to radical group analysis

It is impossible to deal with group analysis and social issues without having to deal with political issues or at least developing an attitude towards political matters. The question is how to tackle them in an academic essay. This is not an easy task, and sometimes it is difficult to separate a scientific analysis from a political position. Using group analysis as a tool for understanding cultural and societal phenomena immediately confronts us with this dilemma.

Although there is a strong political tradition within psycho-analysis, it has been largely washed out by the medicalisation of psychoanalysis in the US. Jacoby (1975) persuasively argues the case that a hallmark of our narcissistic culture is the reduction of all social and collective problems to their psychological component in individual psyches. He uses the term "psychologism". Very simply, Jacoby defines psychologism as "the reduction of social concepts to individual and psychological ones" (p. 78). Problems whose reality is inextricable from their collective and sociological nature are apprehended as individual and psychological problems. Jacoby makes a very convincing case that an alarming characteristic of recent liberal thought has been the tendency to reduce all actions and ideas, all experience and history, to their psychological components.

Many psychologists and psychoanalysts try to refrain from being identified with a definite political attitude, claiming that this will draw them out of the "neutral" analytical stance. Classical psychoanalysis practice was based on the three principles of "anonymity", "neutrality", and "abstinence" (Eagle & Wolitzky, 1992). Cohen, Ettin, and Fidler (1998) have extended this classical psychoanalytic stance to group therapy. Anonymity refers to the therapist's remaining a "blank screen" so as not to interfere with the group members' projections and transference towards the group analyst. It is rarely useful for the analysts to air their political attitude in groups. To this principle we can add the therapist neutrality, meaning that therapists do not take sides in group members' inner or outer conflicts and this includes political conflicts.

This old-fashioned stance kept many psychologists, psychoanalysts, and group analysts from taking a stand and expressing a political point of view. More than that, they became cautious not to be identified with any political party so that they can strictly keep their attitude of neutrality and anonymity. Group analysis, with its focus on the social, perceiving the individual as embedded in culture and its clear implications for society and culture, changes this stand dramatically. Analysing societal phenomena, exploring the social unconscious and describing cultural hidden norms are difficult to achieve from a completely neutral position. An interest in socio-political processes and the social unconscious is usually informed by a sensitive social consciousness. We are always in danger of crossing the line between analysing a social/political situation from a group analytic point of view, and between harnessing the group analytic theory for promoting a political statement. On the other hand, as we are part of the culture and society we analyse, how can we avoid being involved with this object of our research?

Actually, to begin with, Foulkes's idea (1948, p. 10) about the individual as only an abstraction is quite radical. It negates our sense of individual identity and our perception of ourselves as separate entities. Dalal (1998) took this statement further and argued that we cannot isolate an individual from the interpersonal, group or social context. Just as Winnicott dramatically asserted that "there is no such a thing as a baby", because the baby can never be studied outside the dyad of baby–care-giver, Dalal can be paraphrased as saying "there is no such a thing as an individual". According to Dalal (1998), two versions of Foulkesian theory actually exist: Foulkes's orthodox ideas follow Freud and psychoanalytic theory. The orthodox position is usefully extended to include the Gestalt notion of figure-ground relationships, that is, alternating attention to individuals and groups as foreground or background. It seems that this Foulkes had to compromise (or depart from), both theoretically and politically, with the influential psychoanalytic thinking of the time. His radical ideas entail prioritising the group over the individual (consonant with Marxist thinking); the whole over the part (following Gestalt psychology); the social over the biological (in contrast to Freud); the external over the internal (as a counterclaim to Klein and Bion); the social unconscious (or hidden influence of socio-political and cultural constraints) over the Freudian unconscious (as the receptacle of repressed contents), and the mechanism of social transmission over biological inheritance.

So, according to this reading, group analysis is deeply rooted in a radical position. It is tempting to connect the practical and therapeutic aspects of group analysis to conservative-orthodox Foulkes while relating the social implications of this theory to radical Foulkes, but this will be too much of a simplification. In a way, group analysis radical ideas preceded postmodern ideas in which certainties are gone and linear relations between cause and effect are no longer valid. Towards the beginning of the twenty-first century more and more papers appeared in *Group Analysis* connecting this theory to complexity theory (Stacey, 2000), to intersubjectivity (Schulte, 2000), to gender, sexuality, power, and feminism (Burman, 2002), and to class, social status, and inequality (Lauren, 2002).

Perhaps the best paper connecting group analysis to rapid developments in the twentieth century in areas such as political economy, popular culture, personal and sexual relationship, and psychotherapy, is that of Blackwell (2002). He asserts that, like psychoanalysis, group analysis has had to struggle with the tension between being a radical discourse and becoming a respected profession. Economic and ideological emphasis on individualism brought practitioners to neglect the revolutionary ideas at the basis of group analysis. But a mounting dissatisfaction with divided society, fuelled by ideological struggle against racism, sexism, oppression, and cultural imperialism pushed again into the foreground the radical aspects of group analysis, making it a way of understanding and working with groups from families to the whole society. The result of these processes is that the conductor cannot be old-fashionably neutral because she is part of the group matrix, and the researcher using group analytic methods should abandon the belief in the possibility of being neutral in the sense of being objective, because he or she is part of the political system s/he is exploring.

Some core concepts in group analysis

A key concept of group analysis is the matrix. This concept bears the many facets of group analysis because it spreads from the individual into culture. It is derived from the Latin word *mater*, meaning mother, but it also means a womb or a place of creation. Foulkes and Anthony (1965) saw the group as creating the individual, but also as providing him the background. The interplay between figure and ground, creator and created, individual and group/society, is one of the cornerstones of group analysis. The matrix is the mould in which the individual is made. The group matrix is a shaping space enabling growth and development.

Foulkes presented several complementary definitions of the matrix. The most widely cited is:

> The matrix is the hypothetical web of communication and relationship in a given group. It is the common shared ground which ultimately determines the meaning and significance of all events and upon which all communications and interpretations, verbal and non-verbal rest. (Foulkes, 1964, p. 292)

Sometimes the matrix is treated as a kind of "group mind"—although this is a subject of some controversy in group analysis. But to make it more complex, Foulkes (1975) differentiated among three modes of matrix: First there is the *personal matrix*, a complex system of intra-psychic processes. This matrix can be compared to the neuron network in the brain (Foulkes probably developed this notion because he was influenced by Kurt Goldstein, a holistic neurologist with close ties to the Gestalt psychologists; Goldstein had a holistic theory of the human organism, one that challenged reductivist approaches). Then we have the *dynamic matrix*, which is the interrelationship among the group members. This is what creates the group substance and the "group-as-a-whole" phenomenon. We can compare it to hidden fibres connecting individuals in groups, making them into one entity. The last type is the *foundation matrix* which is "based on the biological properties of the species, but also on the culturally firmly embedded values and reactions" (Foulkes, 1975, p. 15). It seems that the founda-tion matrix is a biologically based web, connecting individuals from different cultures, and inside cultures.

Foulkes devoted many writings (e.g., 1975) to core concepts in group analysis, including detailed description of handling therapy group sessions. He describes precisely the room and seating arrange-ments, the circle of chairs (even its size and the kind of low table in its centre), the size of the group (seven to eight), and the duration and frequency of sessions. All these important details are considered the group *setting*. Other group analytic authors followed this tradition writing about the setting of the group (Van der Kleij, 1983), the exter-nal space of the group (Walshe, 1995), etc. Foulkes (1975) referred to the classical principles of conduct required from the patient, such as regularity, punctuality, discretion, abstinence, no outside contact, and no "life" decisions during treatment.

Foulkes was concerned not only with the procedural details of the group setting, but also with their implications for the group work. Although he detailed the provision of the physical space, the marking of the starting and finishing times, the means of communication from outside to the group, and the admission of new members to the group, he referred to them also as the "dynamic administration" of the group. By this term he meant that administrative functions have dynamic meanings: they provide the group with a sense of safety and continu-ity, and enhance a dynamic flow of communication.

Dynamic administration is strongly connected to the maintenance of the group *boundaries*. Boundaries are the interface between the group and the outside world. Managing the boundaries of the group, so as to facilitate an experience of safety and protection, is crucial to the survival of a group as a discrete entity. The capacity to establish and maintain boundaries (the frame of the group) and to organise and manage the setting, are considered core skills essential to the practice of group analysis. A detailed discussion of boundaries and the implications of dynamic administration for the Internet group leader, can be found in Chapter Five.

Internet forums and discussion lists, which are the raw material of this book, present a specific dilemma around their management and dynamic administration. When referring to them as groups (see Weinberg, 2002) we assume that the level of safety in the boundless, virtual world is low since the boundaries of time and space in a discussion group, so typical of a face-to-face analytic group, do not exist. The dynamic administrative function of the forum moderator is crucial in providing this sense of safety. In a boundless, new, unsafe, and unknown environment such as Cyberspace, especially for those inexperienced with technology, this function seems to be the most important characteristic to let the list members feel that someone is taking care of them.

Other important concepts in group analysis are "mirroring" and "resonance". Both terms are unique to the group therapy field. The idea that group psychotherapy is a special field of expertise that needs different concepts than in individual therapy, requiring the learning of special theories and the acquisition of specific skills, is not very common among therapists. Contrary to the above, Foulkes (1964) developed terms and concepts that are unique for groups. Such are the terms of the matrix, resonance, and group mirroring which are the basic constructs of group analysis. Some of Yalom & Lescz's (2005) therapeutic factors, for example, cohesion and universality, are also unique to groups. They will be examined in Chapter Eight in relation to online groups.

Foulkes and Anthony (1965) described the group as *a hall of mirrors*, that is, as a place where the individual can be reflected in many mirrors, through different eyes. According to Roberts and Pines (1991) Foulkes defines the mirror reaction as the "aspect of the self reflected by members of the group through image and behaviour, allowing identification and projective mechanisms, enabling the individual to become aware of these hitherto unconscious elements"

(p. 76). Apparently, it is difficult to detect and experience positive and negative/malignant mirroring processes in online groups. This issue deserves a special attention when talking about groups on the Internet and we will discuss it in depth in the following section.

Although Bion (1959) was not a group analyst, and actually some of his ideas seem to contradict Foulkes's positive connotation of groups, we cannot understand groups without mentioning his important contribution of the three basic assumptions: members of a group often behave as though they are responding collectively to some unconscious and irrational organising principle. Their behaviour may express one of three implicit basic assumptions: dependency, fight–flight, and pairing. For the time being, it is sufficient to say that in almost any group, and Internet groups are no exception, some members' behaviours and irrational group dynamics can easily be explained by these assumptions.

In recent years Hopper (1997) suggested a fourth basic assumption, which is an extension of Bion's (1959) original three basic assumptions. This assumption is expressed in bi-polar forms of incohesion. When activated, groups and group-like social systems oscillate between aggregation and massification. In the massification polarity the group seems unified, members tend to merge with the "group mother" (Scheidlinger, 1974), deny differences and an illusion of togetherness and sameness prevails. In the aggregative polarity, people feel alienated from one another and indifference, hostility and withdrawal from relationships are prevalent. In its extreme form a massive splitting mechanism is active and each subgroup is against each other subgroup. We will see later that this assumption has clear implications to online groups.

We cannot finish this section without mentioning the group *conductor*, although this will also be elaborated upon in a later chapter (Chapter Five) and examined vis-à-vis his/her functions on Internet forums. The group conductor has many functions, such as moving between engagement in the process, reflection, and observation, linking different levels of communication, linking groups, subgroups, and individuals, building a linking structure, paying attention to both process and content, moving between different levels of transference, etc. The analyst has two practical tasks: to enhance the flow of communication within the group boundaries and to attend to events beyond those boundaries. This last task is achieved both by taking charge of the administration of the group's setting and by translating "external material" brought within these boundaries as matter pertaining to the dynamic flow of communication into the "here and now".

Mirror neurons or image neurons?

In a group, it is easier to recognise other people's problems and to consider ways these might be resolved then look directly into one's own problems. Foulkes (1964) calls this the mirror reaction:

> Mirror reactions are characteristically brought out when a number of persons meet and interact. The person sees himself, or part of himself—often a repressed part of himself—reflected in the interactions of other group members. He sees them reacting in the way he does himself, who are in contrast to his own behaviour. He also gets to know himself—and this is a fundamental process in ego development—by the effect he has on others and the picture they form of him (p. 81)

Is mirroring in groups associated to mirror neurons that are lately over-discussed in neurobiology and beyond? Mirror neurons were inadvertently discovered in the early 1990s in Parma, Italy by Giacomo Rizzolati and his team, when a researcher noticed that some brain cells of a Macaque monkey "fire" when the monkey observes the researcher picking up food. These were the same cells that fire when the monkey picks up the food, so the same cells were activated both through motor action and through perception of this same action.

The discovery of mirror neurons ignited the imagination of social scientists and sprouted many hypotheses around their function, from understanding people's intentions, through the development of language, to being the basis for empathy and even playing a role in social skills deficits. Mirror neurons seem to analyse what other people do and to read minds. Mirror neurons and mirror systems provide "hard-wired" support for the group therapist's belief in the centrality of relationships in the treatment process and exploring their value in accounting for group-as-a-whole phenomena. Mirror neurons further confirm the holistic, intersubjective social nature of perception, action, and intention as distinct from a stimulus-response behaviourism. Apparently, mutual identification and recognition precede self-consciousness, reason, and culture. Groupings appear to be a "wired-in" tendency of our species.

We can say that a neuroanatomical basis for empathy and identification appears in view, which is strongly activated in human relationship, let alone in groups, especially when mirror neurons are taken along with the already substantial attention to imitation, affective resonance, and the co-regulation of behaviour and inner states. Further, the emerging model of mirror neuron functioning corresponds to a second feature of the intersubjective core of experience: that as others are encountered, they are simultaneously taken as similar and different from oneself. If we think about it, this is exactly what members of groups explore: similarities and differences. In fact, this is what we do in systems centred group therapy (developed by Agazarian): first help the members create functional subgroups in which people explore how similar they are, and then move to find out where their differences lie (see Gantt, 2012).

Schermer (2010) argues that mirror neurons offer a potential neurological grounding for group-as-a-whole concepts. According to him, these neurons are consistent with self-psychology and the need for empathic attunement, especially in groups (Stone, 2005). He shows that several group therapy theories and concepts go well with these cells. When relating to group analysis, he connects mirror neurons to the group matrix, defined as the communications networks that occur among the group members. Mirror neurons provide a possible link, which connects individuals as "nodal points" to one another. Group analysis emphasises the social nature of the self. Mirror neurons account for the self which defines our individuality.

Because mirroring is primarily based on the ability to look into other people's eyes and be seen by them, mirroring on the Internet seems impossible to achieve due to lack of eye contact. The only concrete reflection people see in Cyberspace is their reflection on the screen. Although the screen can stay an admiring mirror (as the writers can project their ideal-ego on the screen) people need people to be acknowledged. In the large group, mentioned above, at least "auditory mirroring" can replace visual mirroring. On the Internet there is only text. Textual mirroring is possible, but it is more difficult to attain.

From time to time people do feel mirrored in Internet forums, but most of the time their "voice" seems lost in ether. This is quite a narcissistic blow for many people who refrain from raising their voice in the crowd (real or virtual one) in order not to face the painful experience of being ignored. Large and virtual groups supply an example of why people avoid participating in social and political activities, fearing the possibility of being ignored or (worse than that?) even ridiculed. If good citizenship means participating in political activities, enhancing mirroring in the crowd might encourage more people to join.

There are two possibilities of the effect of no mirroring on the Internet. One is that as fewer senses are involved, less shame is evoked. People can still defend themselves with a stronger control of self-boundaries. The writer can decide when to self-disclose, and the typical pressure of the small group and the possibility of intrusion is diminished. On the other hand, people can experience the emptiness and lack of visual cues within Cyberspace as persecutory and find the ambiguities of communication hard to tolerate.

Is empathy possible at all over the Internet? We can argue that as we do not see the other online, it is easier to put him/her in the position of the other—the "not me", and thus feel less empathic and more prone to be involved in acts that have a damaging effect upon other people without feeling guilt or remorse. Lévinas (1984) proposed that our moral responsibility for other people begins where we can see them in front of our eyes. It is through our faces and gazes that we call each other up as human beings. As the Internet most often involves exchanges of only text messages (whether through e-mails, or in Internet forums, listserves, and discussion lists), there is no reason to believe that we would feel morally responsible for someone we do not see and care about the impact of the written words on the person receiving our communication.

Indeed, there are numerous examples of actions of people intending to harm other users on the Internet. In some of them the action is intended to increase the profits of the actor (for example, in Internet frauds) at the expense of innocent people. We can assume that some of these criminals would have not been involved in such illegal acts if they had to cheat on people face-to-face, both because it is easier and safer to do it behind the screen, but also because facing another flesh and blood person activates more moral restraints.

In other cases of evil acts, the harmer does not gain anything financially from the action. For example, spreading viruses on the Internet can affect many people causing their computers to crash and their data to be lost, resulting both in a real damage and a lot of trouble. The people who create and spread these viruses do not seem to care about the suffering of the users, and empathy surely does not seem to be their main motive for their malevolent acts (perhaps a need for power is their drive?).

We do not have to be psychopaths or involved in illegal acts in order to act non-empathically over the Internet. Time and again "normal" people like you and I are drawn into impulsive reactions on Internet groups that do not suit their regular responses in everyday life. We will see later that regression occurs frequently in Internet forums (Holland, 1996) leading to surprisingly aggressive inconsiderate expressions. The reasons for these strange actions are probably the ease of clicking the "send" button with no second thought, and the existence of a faceless other (like the pilot who pushes the button releasing the bomb with no remorse because he cannot see the faces of the people he is targeting). From my own experience, I have learned never to respond immediately to irritating and intriguing messages, but to wait and rethink about an appropriate response, taking into consideration a self-psychological approach that helps me imagine a narcissistically hurt person on the other end of the line. It took me several years of Internet activity to adopt this policy, and I still feel the urge of "showing those bastards who were mean to me" that I can retaliate. Judging from my own self-analysis about what decreases my ability for empathy in such incidents, I assume that it involves the wish not to appear vulnerable, especially in public. As I do not see the other forum members, I project on to them some devaluing attitude towards me after being attacked by someone if I would not retaliate, and thus I am pushed to an impulsive action (the need to "save face" in public).

As mirror neurons are activated when we *see* someone else's behaviour, gestures, or facial expressions, we might conclude that because of the lack of face-to-face interaction on the Internet, these cells are not activated, and this is the neurological cause for the lack of empathy on the Internet. However, at the same time there is evidence for surprising generosity, networks of positive connections and wonderful collaboration among people over the Internet. Holland (1996) included in his description of the Internet regression the fact that people who have never met face-to-face are ready to help one another. As someone involved in group psychotherapy around the world, I receive many requests for articles or references from people I do not know, and I usually find the time to respond and to help them. Other examples of Internet collaboration and networking include helping people we will never meet with useful information, support, acknowledgement, and validation.

We are used to an embodied intimacy between self and others in social relations. We share the same space, which enables us to feel close both physically and psychologically. But if mirror neurons work not only when we interact visually, perhaps shared space can become virtual space? We are misled to believe that mirror neurons are active only when we see the other person's behaviour or gestures. This is probably due to their name (mirror implies visual stimulus) and the fact that their discovery related to seeing (monkeys see, monkeys do). However, Iacoboni (2008) found out that mirror neurons discharge at the mere sound resulting from someone's actions. They code the actions of other people in a multimodal and even abstract way.

In fact, the question is how do we understand people's mental state. Is it by analysing the other person, or by literally pretending to be in other people's shoes. Mirror neurons suggest that the latest hypothesis is true, but in order to do that we do not necessarily need to see the other person. Think about what happens when we read a good novel. We can empathise with the hero, identify with the heroine, feel moved by their actions. We do not see them, but we imagine their actions, feelings, and intensions. This common experience that we all have provides an evidence that mirror (imaginary) neurons fire when we read text as well. Support for this hypothesis comes from Aziz-Zadeh, Wilson, Rizzolatti, and Iacoboni's research (2006) where they asked subjects to read sentences describing hand and mouth actions while measuring their brain activity, and later measuring the brain while showing them video clips of actions. Areas of mirror neurons for hand and mouth movements were also selectively activated while subjects were reading sentences describing these specific actions. Mirror neurons help us understand what we read by internally simulating the action we read. If it happens in a novel (and in that experiment), why not on the Internet?

In my opinion, we can simply imagine the other person acting in order to activate these neurons which help us know the other's state of mind. Imagination is actually visualisation. The imagination is not structured by the eyes alone, and virtual groups stimulate and structure imagination. I am eagerly waiting for the experiment that will confirm this hypothesis that it is enough to imagine other people's actions in order for mirror neurons to fire, just as they do when we see the person acting or act ourselves. I assume that such an experiment will encounter some difficulties, especially regarding the question how to control what people imagine, but I do not see why we cannot try to establish an experiment where we ask subjects to imagine other people acting *vs.* picturesque scenes and measure their mirror neuron activity. If I am right, I suggest changing the misleading name of mirror neurons to imaginary neurons.

Yogev (2012) points out that there are two dimensions of empathy: the non-verbal/facial dimension, related to the attuned gaze, and the verbal dimension involving communication. Certainly, the verbal dimension exists on the Internet, as people can communicate through text and verbally describe what they feel, helping the reader empathise with them. The facial dimension *is* missing on the Internet, and probably this is why it is easier for people to alienate themselves and put their communication partner in the place of the "other". However, as we pointed out earlier, imagining others when we cannot see them can be a close approximation to seeing them, which means that empathy is not totally absent. Mirror neurons work best in real life, when people are face-to-face. Virtual reality and videos might be shadowy substitutes, but they still provide some substitute.

Caring or intruding?

Empathy per se is not enough to guarantee a benevolent behaviour among people. Kohut (see Strozier, 1985) once said that the Nazis were very empathic with the Jews, meaning that they understood the "Jewish mind" so well, that they planned the gas chambers to successfully deceive their victims. The discussion of mirroring and the issue of empathy leads us to more questions: What do people do with their empathy? How do they express this empathy? Do they turn it into care? Which brings to the fore the following common dilemma in human relationship: How can we distinguish between caring for the others and intruding upon their privacy? Where is the thin line we might cross between becoming empathic, wanting to be helpful and between forcing ourselves upon the other, becoming insensitive to one's boundaries? In fact, there is no general answer for these questions, but whenever we become involved in relationship, it is a dilemma that we have to deal with.

In many face-to-face process and therapy groups, this dilemma is part of the group development, and many group members hesitate for a while before showing active curiosity about the other. People are worried that their curiosity will be perceived and sensed as a "Peeping Tom" attitude. Caring is most common and crucial in parent–children relationship. The time parents spend caring for their children and doing basic things for them lays down a crucial substrate for the children's healthy development. It builds up their basic trust and establishes the secure attachments which are the primary condition for future stable relationship. Both partners in this caring relationship benefit from exchange: the children feel that they are loved for what they are, and the parents confirm their capacity to care and love. However, many adults do not want to feel that they need others to care for them, and some reject caring behaviours even when in crisis, fearing that others might pity them in their distress (e.g., when they are terminally ill). For that reason, people withhold expressions of care in groups.

In fact, cultural norms are involved in what is accepted or unaccepted in this dilemma as well. In Israel it is very common to intrude upon one another's boundaries and space, ask rude questions, give unsolicited advice about the right way to behave, etc. In California, where I have lived for the past seven years, people are so respectful of one another's boundaries (from physical and space boundaries to asking personal questions), that sometimes it is felt as an avoidance of connection. Being involved in those two cultures (Israel and California), when I lead groups it is outstanding for me how people in California are hesitant about intruding, and avoid asking personal questions at the beginning stages of the group (and sometimes much later), while Israelis immediately become curious about the other to the extent of disrespecting boundaries.

In my humble opinion, and from my multicultural experience, too much avoidance of curiosity, of being interested in the other and asking questions when someone brings an issue to the group, is felt like lack of caring, isolating the person who started opening up, and creating alienation in the group. On the other hand, too much curiosity and personal questions is experienced as rude, intruding, and disrespectful, creating an unsafe environment in the group.

Facing the above dilemma, here is another online paradox: Internet groups are better in managing these poles, balancing over-curiosity and avoidance of connection, sometimes establishing a culture of care (depending on the right leadership and developing group norms). First, the ability of the person who responds to the personal questions to keep and manage one's boundaries on Internet forums is better than in face-to-face groups, as will be mentioned in Chapter Five. In asynchronous lists, the responder has time to reflect and decide without pressure about the right response and the amount of self-disclosure. Beyond this ability to control one's boundaries, the fact that Internet lists are multicultural results in a balance of the extreme attitudes around curiosity mentioned above, as people learn from one another about what is acceptable in different cultures. More than that, due to developing the illusion of a small group described in Chapter Six, there is a high possibility that people feel more intimate than is expected and participate in a more caring interaction. The presence of the forum leader, intervening in order to maintain a caring group culture, detailed in Chapter Five, is crucial for this process. It is amazing how a group of people that have never met can become a source of support and care for participants in virtual groups. For a comprehensive review of online mental health interventions, including self-help groups, see Barak and Grohol (2011).

Using the frame of reference of group analysis for this book

Usually, qualitative research produces large amounts of textual data in the form of transcripts and observational field notes. The researcher has to make sense of the data by sifting and interpreting them. Data analysis often takes place alongside data collection to allow questions to be refined and new avenues of inquiry to develop. This is exactly the way this research proceeded: the more data that was collected on Internet groups, the more questions and explored areas were developed and refined. The more papers I have written about groups on the Internet, the clearer it became to me just how much a book on this subject is needed. Textual data is typically explored inductively using content analysis to generate categories and explanations. Qualitative research uses analytical categories to describe and explain social phenomena. In order to do that, the researcher needs to identify a thematic framework—key issues, concepts, and themes by which the data can be examined and referenced (Pope, Ziebland, & Mays, 2000). The thematic framework for this book is that of group analysis.

In order to understand the group phenomena in Cyberspace and connect them to questions of cultures and society, I wore the group analytic lens while observing data on Internet forums and discussion lists. I used group analytic terms and concepts to explain my observations and to give meaning to my findings. Relating to the former aspects of group analysis, I moved from analysing individual phenomena to social ones, from small groups to large groups, from the individual unconscious to the social unconscious, always keeping in mind the radical perspective of group analysis.

Conclusion

Group analysis is not merely a form of psychotherapy for individual patients. It moved far beyond the individual, undermining its separate existence, into the study of social processes and cultural phenomena. It begins to emerge as a discourse of both small and large groups, maintaining dialogue over cultures and nations. It also enables members of different cultures to explore their differences and similarities, to study their social unconscious, and understand their cultural identity. It addresses familial, sexual, gender, cultural, and political themes, and provides an opportunity to explore conflicts and contradictions.

> Group analysis, so Foulkes hoped, would provide not only an effective means of psychotherapy, but also an approach to social phenomena, a way of understanding the individual and her society and the relationship between them. It could, he believed, provide a meeting point for psychoanalysis and sociology, for social psychology and anthropology. (Blackwell, 1994, p. 27)

This is what I try to do in this book: using the group analytic frame of reference to analyse culture and social phenomena, to understand the culture of the Internet and its communities, and to connect it to psychoanalytic thinking. I should add that the radical aspect of group analysis assures that sometimes my subjective interpretation of events will guide the analysis.

Group analysis understands interactional processes as playing in a unified mental field of which the individuals composing it are a part. The Internet can be perceived as such a field. In a way, the Internet resembles very much Foulkes (1964) description of the matrix, especially the foundation matrix. If "the matrix is the hypothetical web of communication and relationship in a given group" (Foulkes, 1964, p. 292), than the World Wide Web (WWW) certainly represents such a web. Not only the communication over the Internet creates a web of relationship, but also discussion lists, forums, and listserves allow us to observe how this matrix is interwoven when people connect, respond, resonate, and mirror one another (or fail to do so). We can notice how a group of total strangers coming together into a loose boundary space, share something deep in common, and manifest Foulkes's words:

> I have accepted from the beginning that even this group of total strangers, being of the same species and more narrowly of the same culture, share a fundamental, mental matrix (foundation matrix). To this their closer acquaintance and their intimate exchanges add consistently, so that they also form a current, ever-moving, ever-developing dynamic matrix. (Foulkes, 1973, p. 228)

In addition, group analysis perceives the individual as a nodal point, a sort of intersection in a web, like a neuron in the nervous system. In this way a group, a social system, and society at large is covertly connected. Thus, we are all connected through this incomprehensible web. The WWW itself is an example of such a web, where each item or individual is linked to another item, serving as a nodal point, leading to other links or nodal points, all interconnected together in a deeper foundation matrix.

CHAPTER THREE

Cultures and (virtual) groups: the Internet culture

In a movie titled *The Gods Must Be Crazy* (1980) a Bushman from Africa finds an empty Coca-Cola bottle that someone threw from an airplane, and brings it to his tribe. The Coke bottle that dropped magically from the sky is considered a generous gift of the gods. They have never seen such a useful present that the gods sent them. They use it to pound tubers into mash, to smooth snake skin while curing it, as a stamp to apply decorative ink to leather, and as a musical instrument where you blow across the top to make a whistle. It seems that when people do not know of the original purpose of an object, they make creative uses of it.

But as time goes by the useful present from the gods becomes an evil object for this culture, which so far had no possessions and no ownership. Suddenly everyone is in need for this precious object and unfortunately there is only one bottle. So fights and competition start in this peaceful happy tribe, until finally they decide to get rid of that corrupting object.

This movie story is not only a criticism of the western culture (symbolised by the Coke bottle) but also shows how cultures can be very different from one another. So different that if we try to absorb elements from one culture into another the result might be more harmful than helpful.

In this chapter I would like to discuss Cyberspace culture and its unconscious aspects, and connect it later to Internet groups and forums. But before doing that we should define culture, explore and analyse its distinctive features, and discuss the connection between groups and cultures.

What is culture?

The question of culture can be approached from many perspectives: social, anthropological, psychological, philosophical, and political. Perhaps this is the reason why no agreed definition of "culture" exists and the number of definitions equals the number of writers on this important issue. There is not even a consensus among scholars, philosophers, psychologists, and sociologists as to what exactly the concept should include.

Studying culture involves several aspects that should be explored and analysed (for some cultural studies readers, see Carrithers, 1992; Cole, 1996; Greetz, 1973; Rogoff, 2003). Culture involves what people think, what they do, and the material products they produce. Although definitions of culture vary widely, there is agreement about the following features: The shared aspect of culture means that it is a social phenomenon (Carrithers, 1992), that is it arises when group members share the same norms, values, beliefs, and behavioural patterns (Taylor, 1989). Culture is learned, not biologically inherited, and involves arbitrarily assigned, symbolic meanings of which language is primary (Greetz, 1973). It also includes ways of organising society, from kinship groups, clans, and tribes, to states and multinational conglomerations, and the distinctive formation of groups and their products (Ridley, 1996).

From the conventional arts and media perspectives, culture is associated with different forms of creative expression in the areas of literature, music, drama, etc. It is usually divided between "high culture", relating to the interests of an intellectual elite, and "popular culture", relating to the pleasures and leisure of wider society. Today, references to culture seem to permeate all aspects of society. "Culture", it seems, is implicated in everything we do and everything we are.

Anthropology views culture as defining space, time, health, relationships, rituals, and groups. Bodley (1994), an anthropologist, summarises the following inventory of cultural aspects:

Topical:	Culture consists of everything on a list of topics, or categories, such as social organisation, religion, or economy
Historical:	Culture is social heritage, or tradition, that is passed on to future generations
Behavioural:	Culture is shared, learned human behaviour, a way of life
Normative:	Culture is ideals, values, or rules for living
Functional:	Culture is the way humans solve problems of adapting to the environment or living together
Mental:	Culture is a complex of ideas, or learned habits, that inhibit impulses and distinguish people from animals
Structural:	Culture consists of patterned and interrelated ideas, symbols, or behaviours
Symbolic:	Culture is based on arbitrarily assigned meanings that are shared by a society

From a hermeneutic point of view (Christopher, 2001) culture provides meaning and structure that make social life feasible. Human life is not conceivable without culture because it provides the common understandings that allow the social world to have a meaning. It gives some significance to being a person and provides some understanding of human nature. These "webs of significance" (Geertz, 1973) permeate our social life, practices, institutions, and daily functioning without us even noticing. It is so pervasive that it becomes impossible to separate culture from individuals. We can never fully detach ourselves from the culture we live in because the self is embedded in culture.

From an evolutionist point of view culture is an "adaptation", giving its owner some advantage over alternative forms in the population (Rose, 1997). Culture is helpful to survival and reproduction, because it unites people into groups. Groups of people that collaborate and have some common cultural features uniting them have a better chance to survive than individuals.

Each perspective on culture hides deeper questions and attitudes, especially around the necessity of change or preservation of the current situation as is. All the above aspects have implications regarding the dominant culture and its superiority over other cultures. For example, if culture is a learned social phenomenon, society and its institutions can make use of it to preserve its social classes, gender differentiations, etc. If the self is embedded in a culture that gives meaning to his/her existence, western culture, which stresses individuality and finds significance in self-actualisation, is by no means superior to eastern culture which focuses on tribe or extended family ties and finds meaning in the individual belonging to a larger group.

Psychological aspects of culture

The advantage of culture over individuals is not only in survival. There is a psychological advantage in belonging to a culture. Belonging, in itself, is a basic need and creates a feeling of safety. A member of a specific culture encounters, whether consciously or unconsciously, all the above mentioned patterns, symbols, ideas, and values that make culture what it is. It brings a sense of familiarity and some illusion of certainty in life. Apparently culture has some psychological functions. Kaës (1987) describes four psychic functions of culture:

1. Maintaining the individually undifferentiated basis for psychic structures necessary for belonging to society.
2. Guaranteeing common defences.
3. Enhancing identification and differentiation, which guarantee the continuity of the distinction between the sexes and the generations.
4. Constituting an area of psychic transformation by providing signifiers, representations and modalities for treating and organising psychic reality.

Le Roy (1994) explains that in the first two functions culture contains the undifferentiated aspects of the individual psyche, and in the last two it promotes the structuralisation of the psyche through its introduction into a series of symbolic orders.

Culture protects us from primitive anxieties by structuring the environment and by giving it a meaning. It helps its members to sublimate their impulses and drives, and engage in daily rituals that provide relief from existential anxieties. We know how to deal with life and death through cultural codes and tradition.

Culture is strongly connected to the question of identity. Sometimes when we speak of culture we mean a style of life that is typical or even defines a community or a group people belong to. In this sense it would be better to talk about identity. The sameness of customs, norms, language, dress, code of behaviour, enhances the individual to structure and develop an identity. Erikson (1950) saw ego identity as anchored in a cultural identity. When developing his individual identity the youngster is leaning heavily on the cultural identity, its normative expectations and definitions of what is right. Culture provides the adolescent with a relatively stable environment that helps shape his role in society as well as helping him invest in an identity formation process. When culture changes (such as in migration) this stability is shaken and identity formation is disrupted.

A personal identity cannot be formed without a collective identity to serve as a reference point. Taylor (2002) defines the collective identity as "that descriptive aspect of the self-concept that the individual shares with every member of one's group" (p. 44). Collective identity refers to many group identities and not just the cultural group. It can be based on the professional group people belong to, their neighbourhood, or their constant friends group. But there is something special about the collective identity emerging from culture, because it encompasses almost every area of life. Culture represents the individual's most pervasive and all-inclusive collective identity. Therefore, culture forms the basis for a person's personal identity.

The psychological aspects of culture might explain why is it difficult to analyse culture from a neutral perspective and de-construct its deeper meaning. The psychic structures necessary for belonging to society are threatened when we explore the meaning of culture and its underlying values. Culture seems like a safety envelope that holds together those primitive anxieties mentioned above. Culture stands as a self-evident but often unanalysed entity. Impinging on this imaginary envelope by questioning its basic meaning threatens to undermine society's foundations and set free the anxieties. What will happen to us if we question the distinction between the sexes and the generations?

Culture and awareness

Some cultural dimensions and aspects are quite obvious and people are very aware of them. We are aware of the tradition and habits of the culture we live in. We can easily be aware of the manners and common behaviour that belong to our culture. When we meet people we know we usually greet them in a polite way, and if we fail to do that it looks strange. Language is one of the most important elements of culture, especially if it is unique or endangered. Usually people from a certain culture become more aware of their culture norms when they step out of them and sometimes get the feedback (verbally or just by a rebuking look) that we did something wrong. We know exactly what kind of dress belongs to our culture and can easily identify a person from another culture by the way they dress, even if we never stopped to define our typical cultural code of dressing. (The above sentences assume that culture is unitary. Another possibility is that there might be numerous sub-cultures in a seemingly uniform culture. We will discuss this question later.)

But some of the cultural aspects are more elusive and less obvious. North Americans can be unaware of their individualistic approach, especially if they have never lived in other countries. Israelis might never understand why they are considered rude until they go to Europe and are amazed by the different daily relationships and politeness people display when they relate to one another. Actually, one of the ways to understand one's culture and to become more aware and critical about its features is to look at it from the outside. Only by distancing yourself from your origin and comparing it to other places you might notice that things are different in other places. Another way of becoming aware of hidden cultural codes is by analysing the media, such as TV broadcasts or movies. The mass media represents very well the culture it stems from (On the hidden cultural codes within the media, and how the media synthesise and reproduce them, see Williamson (1988)).

Actually, culture is ubiquitous even without our noticing its presence. It impregnates our daily life and the texture of relationships. As we will see in Chapter Four, about the non-body and presence, culture also constructs our minds and has its impact on our perception and understanding of reality. In that chapter I wrote about the medium of interaction as appearing to be transparent. We can say the same about culture and relate the cultural medium as being invisible. As said there, if reality and presence are socially constructed it means that society and culture covertly and unconsciously mediate every interaction. Culture can be seen as an invisible web standing behind our behaviours and interactions. A culture links its individuals through shared conscious and unconscious assumptions (Sengun, 2001).

As described in the previous chapter, Foulkes (1964) coined the concept of the group matrix, which can be described as the communication network of the group members at both the conscious and unconscious level. Elaborating on the matrix concept Foulkes (1975) further developed the concept of the foundation matrix and the dynamic matrix. The dynamic matrix is still the network of verbal and non-verbal communication in a certain group; dynamic because it undergoes a steady change. The foundation matrix points to the social preconditions enabling group communication to take place. It is "the pre-existing community or communication between the members, founded eventually on the basis that they are all human" (p. 212). It addresses the common ground shared by group members before they enter a group. This means that the foundation matrix connects people from the same culture and speaking the same language. The dynamic matrix is usually portrayed as being superimposed on the foundation matrix and in between are levels that are "transmitted by parents and family in the first place, who in turn transmit the values of what is good, what is bad, etc. in their culture" (p. 213). Thus, the dynamic matrix concept is broadened to include a cultural foundation matrix, which unconsciously and covertly ties and links the individual to society. Among the common grounds allowing the communication among members of the same culture we can count language, cultural and ethical common values, and common interpretation of relationships (including dimensions of gender and generation).

In the past, analytical group therapy discussion hardly dealt with the foundation matrix, maybe because the groups were usually homogenous linguistically and culturally. When therapists stopped working only with middle class homogenous groups of equal native speaker, ethnic, and cultural origin, questions about the foundation matrix started to emerge. We can conclude that as therapists we can be unaware of deep cultural important issues, unless the circumstances change. But can we speak of a more core universal matrix that seems to be lacking in Foulkes's terms and description? This is the matrix connecting people wherever they are based on their common inheritance as human beings. In the current world of globalisation and immigration, we must look further beyond the foundation matrix and ask questions about this core matrix. We might find out (as we do in multiculturally composed groups) that the differentiation into cultures that we are used to, is not so self-evident, and that more basic tenets unite people rather than separate them. This is one of the potentials of the Internet culture: to enable exploring this core matrix.

Culture surrounds us in invisible ties. The process of the psychic development of the individual is embedded in the dominant culture, but the person is unaware of its existence in everyday life or at least its heterogeneity. Culture impacts our eating customs, bodily contacts, child rearing patterns, and relationship to time, space, and the other, but it is always there in the background unnoticed. It is especially difficult for people from a dominant majority group to notice their invisible values and codes of behaviour because they often take for granted their practices as the norm (Perry, 2001). For example, North Americans going to international conferences have difficulty understanding that the use of English excludes others and is an advantage and even a powerful position for them over others. The most difficult cultural processes to examine are the ones that are based on unquestioned tacit basic assumptions. One of them is the presumption of the homogeneity of cultures. Only points of tension/conflict prompt awareness of diverse sub-cultures, for example, around gender, class, sexuality, or dominant/minority cultural status. As we saw earlier, one of the key tenets of group analysis is to acknowledge and work with these tensions.

Cultural processes surround us involving subtle, tacit, taken-for-granted ways of doing things (Rogoff, 2003). For example, a member of a majority group is usually unaware of the privileges this social group belonging bestows. Even information processing is influenced by the social minority-majority contexts (Turner, Hogg, Oakes, Reicher, & Wetherell, 1987) whereas members of majorities tend to perceive more homogeneity in the outgroup than in the ingroup, members of minorities often show the opposite tendency. Perhaps the way to become aware of the tiny numerous culture mechanisms that hold our reality together is to create some estrangement of daily routine and make it less taken for granted. Distancing ourselves from what is usually comprehensible enables us to suddenly see what evades our eyes regularly. In order to do this we should get rid of ethnocentrism and be able to adopt an outsider perspective of our community. In a way the Internet provides us with such an estrangement and distancing. It not only provides a meeting space for different cultures, encountering people with their daily beliefs, but also shapes a new culture in a seemingly egalitarian environment. That is why studying groups in Cyberspace supplies us with invaluable information about the creation of a new culture through the assembly of people from all over the world.

The idea of the social unconscious (Hopper & Weinberg, 2011) is strongly related to the question of how much we are aware of the invisible cultural constraints that surround us. Actually we can see the cultural areas we are unaware of as part of the social unconscious (although it is much more than these areas). We will discuss the social unconscious in Chapter Seven.

Culture and oppression

We are born into a culture, introjecting its norms from early infancy. We are first introduced to the family culture, which in itself is embedded in the social world. We cannot escape internalising cultural codes as we grow up: how to dress, how to behave, how to speak, what is correct, and what is wrong. From the moment of birth we are surrounded by cultural symbols, messages, and values that become part of our social identity. So even though western liberal thinking subscribes to notions of free will whereby we imagine we can choose which behaviour suits us, actually these behaviours vary along quite a limited range. The fact that we are not aware of those invisible cultural ties facilitates the illusion that we are free to choose what to wear and how to speak. In reality, culture is a golden cage. It is golden because it offers many advantages for those who obey its hidden code. As said before, culture is essential for survival, bringing a sense of belonging, granting meaning to life, soothing deep anxieties, etc. Only when people behave in contrast to cultural norms are they are surprised to receive censoring reactions. They suddenly realise how entrapped they were in an unconscious pattern.

Belonging to a group triggers a conflict that has its echoes in being part of a culture. On the one hand members want to be part of the group (community, culture), and thus fulfil their needs for belonging and not feeling lonely. On the other hand in order to belong to the group, the individual has to give up some of his/her separateness and uniqueness by conforming to the norms. According to Mackenzie &

Livesley (1983) this dilemma appears in the first stage of a group life, but actually might only be stronger or clearer at the beginning and it continues to linger in the background as long as the member belongs to the group. In his *Civilisation and Its Discontents*, Freud (1930a) had already discussed the individual as caught in a struggle between the demands of culture and "civilisation" and the pleasure principle. Freud argued that there was a conflict between our id or instinctual nature and the requirements of civilisation. We can apply his argument to every culture or group. This struggle, which is inevitable and fundamentally never resolved, is a necessary part of being part of a culture.

Awareness itself is not always enough to free ourselves from the hidden chains of cultural oppression, although sometimes it is a necessary step. Marginalised and minority groups internalise their social status and the negative attitude towards them, resulting in a lower self-esteem. Disadvantaged groups still tend to use "depressed entitlement" (Jost, 1997) and low status groups still show out-group favouritism (Sidanius & Prato, 1999) despite the enormous development in strengthening favourable social identities and empowering minority groups. An extreme example is the case of women surviving domestic violence. They have been subject to social isolation, but paradoxically when they escape to secret refuges they are even more isolated and marginalised (Burman, 2004). It is not only their own inner dynamics influencing this process, but also an institutionalised social solution, keeping this marginalised oppressed minority group more isolated, despite the good intentions and social awareness of the helping services.

The Internet appeals to many people because it seems as a culture freer than any other culture. People are free to create their own identity, play whatever role they want to present, change their gender and at the same time disclose very intimate information about themselves. On the surface it looks as if the Internet is the ultimate democracy, where each person has an equal status and ability to influence, and with no gender, race or ethnic bias. A more thorough exploration shatters this simplistic notion. In relating to gender issues, for example, there are two opposing approaches to Cyberfeminism. Researchers such as Plant (1997) argue that women are becoming liberated from the traditional patriarchal power structures that surround and engulf them. In turn, gender roles and gender identity are breaking down, where our societal notions of being human, feminine, and masculine are in transition. Others criticise this "net utopianism" claiming that information exchange on the Internet does not automatically obliterate hierarchies, and fear that Cyberspace will simply recreate the same old stereotypes of gender identity, given that it too is structured by capitalist and patriarchal social relations.

Psychoanalysis and psychotherapy are supposed to be free from moral judgment and culturally unbiased. They are not. I dare say that they cannot be. Freud wanted to base psychoanalysis on a pure scientific basis, and put the psychoanalyst in an objective role. Many theoreticians criticised this point of view. For example, his equating femininity with passivity was vigorously attacked by many feminists (Benjamin, 1998). In fact, Freud was entrapped in the cultural norms of his time and place, and even though he was revolutionary in relation to sexuality, he could not free his mind from cultural ties when it came to gender issues. His dichotomy and binary approach to doctor and patient, object and subject, male and female were deeply influenced by the hierarchical views of the end of the nineteen century (Frosh, 1999). It took almost a century to transform psychoanalysis into an intersubjective experience, and what probably contributed mostly was the postmodern zeitgeist with its deconstruction of any binary terms (see Aron & Starr, 2013) and flat structures of systems. Just as the feminist discourse has pointed out that the public language has been a way of putting women and other minority groups "in place", we can claim that psychoanalytic language is acting as the formal dominant-controlling culture in the psychotherapeutic field.

Is culture a unity? Relations between groups and culture

Studying culture poses the question of whether we can treat it as a monolithic entity. When people belong to the same culture we assume some uniformity of behaviour and ways of thought. This is a questionable assumption and might become a dangerously misleading over-generalisation. Being an American means belonging to the American culture, but does it mean that a Californian and a New Yorker have similar norms and codes of behaviour just because they are both Americans? Or is a Muslim from Iran the same as a Muslim from Morocco? And if s/he is similar, what might the continuity across diverse cultural contexts mean? We might even question the existence of a unitary Cyber culture encompassing the behaviour and attitudes of all the members in an Internet community. The closer one looks the more likely one is to discern differences within groups, and the splitting of groups into subgroups can go on ad infinitum. In a way this problem has echoes with the different layers of the matrix mentioned earlier, as the core matrix connects all humans while the cultural foundation matrix (defined earlier) is the hidden network for a certain society and the group matrix are the covert fibres binding a certain group.

Why, then, do people assume homogeneity of culture? We can learn from the way groups (try not to) deal with diversity through an avoidant strategy that overemphasises sameness. This strategy is invoked when archaic anxieties are triggered. These groups might ignore differences around gender, class, sexuality, or underprivileged minorities. Many group experts referred to the shared illusion of group members about the existence of a group entity that keeps the group's cohesiveness. Anzieu (1984) called it "the group object", Segalla (1996) termed it "the group self-object", Karterud (1998) named it "the group self", and Cohen (2002)—"the group's self". In a similar way there is a need for people to imagine an envelope-unitary culture that maintains the cohesion, identity and safety of the individual and groups within this culture. Just like in groups, they also ignore diverse sub-cultures.

Discourses of culture have historically and currently appeared to be deeply connected with notions of "same" and "different". The issue involves the question of how differences come to be viewed as such, and which remain "unmarked" through being part of a dominant culture, and so are normalised into invisibility. We are all aware of the stereotyped-racist notion in western culture that "all Japanese (Chinese, Blacks, whatever) look alike". Phoenix (1987) discussed the ways black women are represented in academic discourses as a normalised absence/pathologised presence. This attitude towards a minority group denies differences among that group, and easily leads to stereotyping and pathologising minority groups. Some ways of thinking about difference deny overlap and intersection in ways that foster affirmations of absolute difference. For example, Israelis tend to relate to Arabs living in Israel as a united block, not differentiating between Muslim Arabs and Christian ones, who are enormously different. This is an easy way for Israelis to protect themselves from a (realistic or imagined) danger and put all the "suspected enemies" in the same basket. Similarly foreign workers in most countries are treated as a crystallised unity (even though they might come from very different cultures), which makes it easy to treat them as a marginalised minority group. So in some contexts fostering affirmations of absolute difference might contribute to racism and apartheid.

If we take the matter of cultural differences seriously, we can conclude that people coming from different cultures have different psychologies and different psyches. This conclusion presumes internalisation of the cultural forces into the individual's psyche. We should bear in mind that individuals and culture are inseparable and that development of the person is intertwined with the person's culture. Having said the above, we risk the danger of justifying racism. Dalal (1998) offers a critique of the ways in which different psychologies are attributed to different cultures, and provides a set of other conceptual tools for thinking about difference, in ways that are not mutually exclusive. He goes further to warn about the dangers of attributing different psychologies to different cultures, because it leads to racism and apartheid (p. 208). This might become true if we confuse differences with worthiness or value. The fact that people from different cultures differ (either inside or outside) does not make them better or worse. Denial of differences out of fear of racism is like throwing the baby out with the bath water.

Let us take as an example the differentiation that Hall (1976) is making between individualistic and collective cultures. Individualistic cultures are guilt provoking cultures: members who do not follow their culture norms and rules tend to feel guilty. Their personal conscience (which is the internalisation of social norms) functions as an internal guide for their behaviour. Collective cultures are shame-ridden cultures. A deviation from expected behaviour evokes shame not only in the individual, but the entire group feels ashamed. This might be a useful analysis, but is it not an over-generalisation? Another example is the four cultural dimensions as suggested by Hofstede (2001), that is widely used in multi-cultural research: individualism-collectivism, uncertainty avoidance, power distance, and masculinity-femininity: Although these are not dichotomies, we can still arrange different cultures along the continuum of these axes.

Does it imply that all people from the East are collectivists, or that all Latin American people can tolerate uncertainty and so forth? Although one can argue that this sort of gross division between the cultures is useless because it is too general, it still describes well the general principles and motives for the behaviour of people from different cultures (see Weinberg, 2003a).

A possible solution is to describe individuals' participation in cultural communities instead of thinking of culture as consisting of separate categories (Rogoff, 2003). Cultural features can be treated as interdependent aspects of multifaceted pattern. As the individual belongs to many communities which overlap, we cannot talk separately about one's belonging to a specific culture. Community can be defined as a group of people who have some common and continuing values, interests, understanding, history, and practices. This does not mean that people from the same community have precisely the same point of view or share the same interests. So Americans can share some common features and still be very different according to their ethnic origin. This solution can also answer the above question about the Internet non-monolithic feature. People can belong to an Internet community but still not share exactly the same values or perspectives. They belong to other communities and cultures outside the Internet, which none the less have their influence on their lives.

Ridley (1996) argues that society and culture exist to bind and cohere groups together. His point of view is biological and based on the evolutionary assumption that groups of people that collaborate survive better than the isolated individual. Elias (1989) reaches the same conclusions from a sociological standpoint. He claims that a sense of cohesion develops over time in the family, based on a stock of common memories, attachments, and dislikes.

So if we agree that groups are essential to human development and that people relate themselves to groups, the question is: to what group or groups? This brings back the issue of identity and the multitude of potential identities. At first it seems that the question is where to draw the imaginary boundary between one group and another. It is easier when two groups have seemingly distinctive cultural and physical features and clear differences (such as North Americans and Japanese), but most of the time groups overlap in many features, and they might be different along one distinct dimension while looking similar in other dimensions. In many cases the distinction into "us" and "them" is just an easy way to simplify and split reality into more comprehensible categories. Actually, when people from groups who look so different are ready to really talk to one another, strange things happen. If they are ready to change an ideological discussion (meaning that there is only one truth and it is the ideology of my group) into discourse/dialogue (meaning that it is not an external reality but a self-referential one), they find out that they have much more in common than they thought.

Of course language is a key medium of cultural identity/difference and is still left as an impassable barrier. People from different language speaking cultures will always feel less privileged and weakened when forced to speak in their dialogue-partner's language. On the surface it looks as if language is the ultimate boundary clearly differentiating cultures, and unconsciously becoming the instrument of oppression for the dominant culture. For example, the fact that Internet communication is mostly conducted in English is on the one hand trying to unify the Internet into a homogenous culture, it also gives an enormous advantage to English speakers, and excludes people who do not speak this language. But when we turn into the spoken-heard language, we find out that not all English-speakers have the same accent. Not only that Americans, Australians, and British sound different, but even inside the UK or the US people from different regions can be identified according to their particular pronunciation of words. So language too, that seemed as setting the boundaries for cultures is again fragmented when delving with the different groups that belong to that same-language-speaking culture.

We can use the term "group" as "a collection of people who interact with one another as parts of a social system . . . .. Each has its own culturally defined goals, roles, rules of procedure, and leadership style'" (Cohen, Ettin, & Fidler, 2002, p. 182). This way groups are connected to culture already through their definition.

Groups develop and have their own cultures.

> We could say there is the internal (intrapsychic) culture, the family culture, the subgroup culture (psychologists, military, list-members), and the social culture (US, Israel), etc. If the group members come from the same social culture, the developing group culture can replace the values and norms of the original culture of the group members. (Weinberg, 2003a, p. 264)

Sometimes the norms and behavioural patterns of groups reflect the culture of the larger communities. Other times smaller groups and larger groups' culture is interchangeable, or at least it is impossible to determine who impacts whom. Take the case of the family, for example. A family is a group too, which has its habits, ways of relating to the world, child rearing patterns, gender roles, and practices. A certain culture can be deduced when many families from the same community behave similarly. At the same time families have their own unique culture that does not reflect the outside urban, ethnic, or national culture. Culture can include many groups all of which share some common values. The group boundaries are more clearly defined than cultural boundaries. Culture is a more abstract entity than a specific group that usually includes a definite number of people. There is a lack of terms in which to discuss groups and culture at the same time, without betraying the complexity and the depth or the influence of either.

Therapy and process groups have a culture of their own too. "A psychotherapy group is a small temporary society with a therapeutic purpose, so this experience of the group is a cultural experience" (Jacobson, 1989, p. 476). But contrary to natural groups such as families, this culture develops along these groups' lifetime. If we see the group as a microcosm we might learn from the development of the group culture about the development of wider cultures. Cohen, Ettin, and Fidler (2002) tried to do this by applying group processes to political problems. They even ambitiously mapped political systems onto their process group analogies, crowning democracy and its culture as the most developed group stage based on independent and interdependent forms of human governance. Alternatively, Jacobson (1989) uses Bion's (1959) ideas about the basic assumptions that develop in the group to describe the creation of a fantasised unitary "group" entity that is distinct from the collection of individuals in the room. This "group" becomes an object in the cultural field. Cultural objects like this "group" are ubiquitous in linking individuals to their groups. As he puts it, "It is one of those things via which we relate to larger groups of which we are a part, and which are important to our experience of ourselves as members of the group" (Jacobson, 1989, pp. 492–493).

The Internet culture: we-ness, me-ness, and in-betweeness

In Chapter One I pointed out that the Internet allows for less committed relationships and that in Internet forums, control over the amount of involvement is not only possible, but also much more accepted and expected. In fact, I even suggested that the ebb and flow of involvement in an Internet forum is a normal part of its existence. Let us now deepen our understanding of this feature from the point of view of the Internet culture.

According to Brewer (1991) people are driven by two conflicting needs: the need to express their individuality and uniqueness, *vs*. the need to belong to a larger meaningful and significant group. We can talk about two separate identities: The collective identity (defined earlier by Taylor, 2002) of belonging to the large group, and the interpersonal identity that relates to the individual in relation to other people. Actually, in both cases the person identifies his/her identity in relation to others, either as part of a large group or as an individual. However, these two needs seem contradictory, and fulfilling one of them arouses the need to fulfil the other as well. People strive to belong to a group that fulfils both these needs in an optimal way.

The conflict between me-ness (the need to "cling" to one's separate individuality and to answer one's narcissistic needs, sometimes at the expense of the community needs) and between we-ness (the need to belong to community or to a larger entity and give up some of one's narcissistic needs) exists in any level we examine. As pointed out in the first chapter, in any relationship the individual gives up some personal freedom. Close relationship means some caring for the other (or investing in fulfilling the other's needs) in exchange for being taken care of by the other, hoping for a balanced and reciprocal relationship. This conflict reveals itself in any higher level of system organisation such as families, small group, community, large group, and social/political/national group.

In its extreme manifestation, holding an unbalanced position between me-ness and we-ness is problematic and even pathological. On the personality level, avoiding any belonging to a relationship can express itself as a schizoid personality disorder, and taking care only of one's needs while ignoring the others can manifest itself in a narcissistic personality disorder. On the social level, an extreme approach of ignoring the needs of another social (or national) group can lead to segregation, racism, or nationalism. Fundamentalism can be seen as an example for such a situation when the religious values of the group are considered as the only truth and demand a strict adherence to specific theological doctrines.

Foulkes, the father of group analysis, was highly interested in the dilemma of individuality and society. As in many other areas, he swings between the orthodox approach and the radical one. In the first issue of the *Journal of Group Analysis* (1967), he is on the one hand fascinated by the white ants who are only apparently individuals but actually are connected in invisible bonds. As if feeling that he went too far comparing them to mankind, he withdraws and says: "Naturally these circumstances cannot and should not be transported to human beings who especially in Western modern society very much feel themselves to be independent individuals."

In Cyberspace, one can both keep individuality on the one hand while belonging to an Internet group on the other hand, and without feeling the compromise people usually feel when they join a community and have to give up some of their freedom. The contrast between our need to belong and our need for autonomy and independence seem to disappear or at least soften in virtual space. The fact that it is possible to have your cake and eat it too on the Internet might mean that although the tension between "me-ness" and "we-ness" is usually felt as two poles of the same axis, actually these dimensions represent two orthogonal axes, and one can find a way to "score" high on both dimensions at the same time. It means that we can actually keep our sense of individual self and subjectivity, while feeling connected and belong to a family, group, large group, society, or nation.

Kohot (1971) described the self as developing separation of self from other along two developmental lines. One is the object-love axis (where one becomes more differentiated and perceives the other as separate) and the other is the healthy narcissistic axis (where more mature and abstract transformations of self-object needs appear). These axes develop in a parallel way. Similarly, we can talk about developing mature ways of maintaining one's subjectivity and individuality without becoming unhealthily narcissistic or isolated, and at the same time, developing mature group belonging and cohesiveness with merging or losing one's boundaries.

Several scholars were struggling with this issue of "me-ness" and "we-ness" as related to trauma and large group processes in the late 1980s. Turquet (1975) suggested a fourth basic assumption in addition to Bion's famous three basic assumptions in groups. He termed this assumption as "oneness", when people in a group tend to lose their sense of individuality and merge into one mass. On the other end of this axis, Lawrence, Bain, and Gould (1996) suggested a fifth basic assumption which they termed "me-ness". In this group situation people fortress their individual boundaries and become only immersed in their own narcissistic needs. Hopper (1997) suggested that trauma is recapitulated in large groups and conceptualised his fourth basic assumption of massificatioin/aggregation in which groups and group-like social systems oscillate between the two poles. In the aggregative polarity, people feel alienated from one another. Indifference, hostility, and withdrawal from relationships are prevalent. In the massification polarity, denial of differences and an illusion of togetherness and sameness prevails. We will return to explore this basic assumption in the next chapters.

In any group, especially in a large group, specifically in society, we must struggle to maintain both diversity and unity. Diversity should not be confused with aggregation and unity should not lead to massification. The Internet culture allows for both a sense of diversity (where else can we find such a diverse expression of voices, individuals, cultures, and even languages living together?) and a sense of unity at the same time (we all belong to this world-wide-web and feel a sense of connectedness to one another). It is the ultimate culture that enhances both a healthy, non-extreme sense of "me-ness" and "we-ness", resulting in what we can call "in-betweeness".

CHAPTER FOUR

The non-body on the Internet: presence, immediacy, subjects, and (group) therapy

Introduction

One of the common arguments, perceiving Internet connections negatively, is that these are "virtual" relationships, totally different from the "normal" way that people connect face-to-face. People are used to embodied, body-to-body relationships, and relate to non-body contact as strange and "not natural". Therefore, before continuing the discussion about relationship and groups on the Internet, we should deal with the common criticism about Internet interaction that argues that such a relationship is not real because no one is physically present in Cyberspace.

The Internet is revolutionary not only because of the way people connect with one another or retrieve information, but also because of the philosophical and psychological premises that reside behind it. The non-existence of the body in Cyberspace enables exploration of postmodern ideas that so far has had no way of being tested. The ability people have on-line to create different characters, play several roles, change their age, and/or appear as another gender was perceived as problematic and even dangerous by some psychologists, but clearly demonstrate the multi-facets of the self and of subjectivity.

It seems that without being connected to their bodies people can explore more possibilities of the self and their subjective experience in ways that were blocked for them before the Internet era. It brings an "understanding of human subjectivity . . . as a partial, polymorphous and adaptable phenomenon" (Sey, 1999, p. 26).

The existence of a multi-self as a healthy and natural way of being is one of the main premises of the intersubjective and relational approaches in psychology (see Mitchell, 1993). Although people tend to sense that they have a singular, true self, and experience themselves as containing (or being) a one "self" that comes with a feeling of presence, integrity, and fullness—this self can change in different circumstances, with different people and in different situations. Mitchell (1993, pp. 114–115) writes: "the portrayals of self as multiple and discontinuous and of self as integral, and separable seems to be at odds, mutually exclusive. They are not. People act both discontinuously and continuously." Bromberg (1996) is another writer advocating the coexistence of "multiple versions of the self". He concludes that they represent crystallisations of different interactional schemes, and that this multiplicity may also signal the existence of an inner, functional limit on the process of self-integration.

The use of different languages can indicate differences in the structure of the self. Studies of bilingual patients showed that different languages reflect very different self organisations (Foster, 1992). The problem is that in everyday life there is no way of experimenting with different self states, and those expressing their different self organisations overtly are labelled with dissociative identity disorder (DID). The Internet is a legitimate and perhaps the only way to explore the multiple self.

In her book *Life On the Screen* (1995) Turkle describes how, in the late 1960s and early 1970s, she lived in France in a culture that taught "that the self is constituted by and through language, the sexual congress is the exchange of signifiers, and that each of us is a multiplicity of parts, fragments and desiring connections" (p. 14). These ideas (of Lacan and Derrida, for example) seemed like inspiring abstractions that had nothing to do with everyday life. The embodiment of the self in ordinary life prevented people from having any access to experiencing their selves the way those philosophers and psychoanalysts described—as a decentred self. There was no way for ordinary people to have an experience that will materialise the idea that the unitary self is an illusion. Turkle

(1995) describes the Internet experience, accessing MUDs (Multi User Dimension: a multiplayer real-time virtual world using role playing games), participating in a virtual community, chatting on-line, etc., as providing such an experience for the crowd.

This revolution changes our ways of thinking not only about the self but also about relationship, intimacy and human connectedness. The possibility of relations that do not involve the body might be confusing, but it also enables a new understanding of connection. It is a connection between selves, partial and decentred as they are.

The new understanding of relationship cannot pass by without having a serious impact on psychotherapy. Whether we talk of individual, couple, family, or group therapy, we imagine people sitting next to one another, seeing each other, hearing the others' voices, and feeling the therapist as present physically, emotionally, and psychologically. What happens if we take away the bodies and move to Cyberpsychotherapy?

In fact, classical psychoanalysis provides a setting that is not so detached from the one described above, since lying on the couch, with the analyst behind the patient, creates some of the conditions that exist in therapy over the Internet when the therapist is not seen. The question might become in what ways does relationship (or therapy) change when other senses are removed from the interaction, sometimes leaving only text as a means of communication. Actually, this is what happened when moving from individual psychoanalysis to group analysis. Scholz (2011) points out that, like Freud, Foulkes's innovation first was a methodological one: he changed the setting— from the couch to the circle. The rule of free association thus was changed to that of free discussion. And Foulkes was very much aware of the fact that changing the setting required a change in theory. Maybe the change to Cybertherapy needs a change in theory as well?

Perhaps instead of insisting that online interaction, and online therapy, is not "real" interaction, we should first understand what do people mean when they talk about "real" relationship and "real" presence?

What is presence?

Most of the traditional views relate to "presence" as involving the body. Actually, covert norms of relationship and communication in western society presuppose the co-presence of two bodies in the inter-action. These cultural hidden norms have structured the notions of individual-society relation, and even conceptions of subjectivity. Two embodied subjects meet in order to interact, communicate, and make a relationship. Accordingly, this metaphysics of "presence" structures most therapeutic approaches, and consequently devaluates "medi-ated" (non face-to-face) encounters. Turkle (1995) interviewed students who suggested that computers would need bodies in order to be empathic, and need to grow up with attachments in order to feel pain. In fact, these attitudes reflect their images of therapy.

Conventional counselling and therapy covertly emphasise a face-to-face, real time interaction. Most of them see the relationship between the therapist and the client as the most significant element in therapy, and value authenticity as one of the "healthy" ways of being in the world. Cyberspace and its implications severely undermine this most common connotation of "presence". By doing this they challenge most psychotherapies who rely on a face-to-face interaction.

Let us return to the group-analytic concept of "the matrix" we presented in one of the previous chapters. The matrix is what connects people together in various situations. It is the communication web in a group (the dynamic matrix), but also the connectedness of people in society (the foundation matrix). Powell (1991) argues that we can delineate the matrix as either inside us or outside us. The inside matrix is the embodied matrix and is susceptible to psychobiological investigation. On the other end there is also the outside unembodied matrix which encompasses the nature of the transpersonal mind (this consists of the social unconscious). This matrix is not based on the existence of human bodies and refers to a relational interface.

Does "presence" necessitate a body? The human body materialises itself in two emotionally laden features that define presence in general: voice and look. The presence of the other is felt through hear-ing the other's voice and seeing the other's body features. The fact that the other looks at us and talks to us causes us to feel present and "seen". Usually this is one of the ways "mirroring" can be achieved in a group (Weinberg & Toder, 2004): people observe other members in the group and see their own behaviour reflected through the other. Another aspect of the look and the voice is its authoritative oppressive function. These functions originate in God's act as the founder of the world. When God "said", creatures were created. When God "saw", people felt they could not escape justice. So looking and saying can also become powerful tools of enslaving the other. We can say that voice and look participate in being present and in connection in a double fold way: a benign one (e.g., being seen and mirrored by the other) and a malignant one (being oppressed by the other's look). Perhaps internet communication frees the participants from this oppressive aspect?

The voice in the psychoanalytic-Lacanian approach is the expression of subjectivity. Expressing one's unique voice is an important indication of having individual thoughts, ideas and feelings. A silent member of a group or society can easily be ignored and related as inexistent. Social minority groups are keenly aware of this lesson and do their best to be heard, sometimes even through explosive sounds when they are desperate. In a large group sometimes people feel intimidated and the words are "stuck in their throats". In an atmosphere of emotional isolation and anonymity they might feel a threat to one's identity, individuality, and subjectivity (Freud, 1921c; Turquet, 1975). The crowd seems to devour and swallow the subjectivity of the individual. When a participant in the large group expresses her voice for the first time she feels quite a relief as if acknowledging her existence (Weinberg & Schneider, 2003).

The voice of the other brings to our attention the fact that others exist too. So awareness to the presence of the other and sometimes to his or her uniqueness and specific needs awakes by hearing their voice. At the same time opening one's eyes activates awareness too. In the book of Genesis, after Adam and Eve ate from the Tree of Knowledge their eyes opened and they became aware of their nakedness. Awareness to ones nakedness and vulnerabilities brings shame and fear, but can also become a vehicle and an engine for progress. Western society and civilization achievements are partly the result of becoming aware of human vulnerabilities and weaknesses and trying to overcome them.

The existence of an observer is what differentiates between an object and a subject. Indeed, this sets up the boundary between the object and the subject. It also distinguishes between enslaver and enslaved, oppressor and oppressed. This might become a basic fault in any therapy, because the therapist (object) who is always looking, seeing, analysing and interpreting the patient (subject) is always in an authoritarian (oppressive) position. He has the power, she knows the "truth", she is "the object who is supposed to know it all." Possibly, that is why post-modern approaches in psychoanalysis present themselves as inter-subjective in nature. They try to change the power structure in therapy by positioning two subjects who interact in the therapeutic session, with each of them impacting the other. This is a more balanced view of the therapeutic relationship. Foulkes might have been aware of this difficulty too when defining group analysis as "a form of psychotherapy by the group, of the group, including its conductor" (Foulkes, 1975, p. 3). Including the conductor in the analysis softens the power position of the group leader, as his interventions are prone to analysis as well. Is it possible that the Internet creates the same revolution because it usually lacks voice and sight, and this way breaks down the definition of subject and object?

As technology advances, communication becomes more and more mediated. It becomes virtual and lacks some "real presence" features. In phone conversations the face of the speaker is absent, but the voice is still loudly present. TV broadcasts transmit sound and picture, but the observer cannot touch or smell the speaker. The Internet brings part-communication to its extreme. It lacks all features and cues but text. It is the prototype of "indirect", mediated communication.

But does unmediated communication really exist? We are used to thinking that a face-to-face interaction is an unmediated one. It is, only if we disregard the air that separates between the speakers, and if we ignore the space and the distance between their bodies. The fundamental Western belief is that speaking and thinking are co-present and that speaking is immediate. Writing is supposed to be the substitute for the immediacy of the voice and represents the non-presence. Derrida (1974) opposes this common view and argues that speech is already inhabited by writing and hence is mediated and derivative. Derrida's ideas receive their utmost expression on the Internet, where writing is the common way of communication, but is experienced by most authors who exchange e-mails or chat in chat rooms as "talking".

Different aspects of presence

So what is presence? Schloerb (1995) defines physical presence as "the existence of an object in some particular region of space and time" (p. 68). Still he believes that an aspect of physical presence, which is causal interaction, does not necessarily require physical presence. He also adds that physical presence supports subjective presence. According to Lombard and Ditton (1997) there are six conceptualisations of presence in relevant literature. All of them lead to a definition of presence as "the perceptual illusion of non-mediation". A summary of their concept explication follows with its implication to therapy and Cyberspace.

Presence as social richness

In organisational communication presence is the extent to which a medium is perceived as sociable, warm, sensitive, personal or intimate when it is used to interact with other people. The more someone is transmitting warmth, sensitivity, and creates an atmosphere of intimacy, the more this person is perceived as present in relationship. In most therapies, the therapist is supposed to be warm and sensitive towards the client. Failure to do so will result in a feeling of alienation for the client, and maybe in ending therapy. In the self-psychological frame of reference, for example, this non-presence of the therapist might be termed as an empathic failure. Other psychotherapeutic approaches, such as Rogerian or Existential, stress the importance of acceptance and close relationship in therapy.

We are so used to thinking about this social richness as possible only in face-to-face relationship, that it is hard to believe that Internet connection can create the same impression. Actually, even TV broadcasters can transmit this "presence" through the TV screen, and their observers discuss their appearance as more or less "warm". Small wonder that McKenna, Green, and Gleason (2002) concluded (and showed) that, "relationships will develop closeness and intimacy significantly faster over the Internet than will relationships begun off-line, because of the greater ease of self-disclosure, as well as the founding of the relationship on more substantive bases, such as shared interest" (p. 11).

This aspect of presence is related to two important concepts implied to non-mediated interpersonal communication: intimacy and immediacy (Argyle & Dean, 1965). Intimacy was mentioned already above (and will be discussed in depth later) and is no doubt possible in Cyberspace. How about immediacy?

In therapy and especially group therapy, immediacy is a term mostly used in the modern group analysis approach. Ormont (1996) explained that striving for immediacy in group therapy means that, "we want the members to experience themselves and others exactly as they are in the moment" (p. 39). The immediacy concept in groups and relationship is strongly related to the "here-and-now" experience, focusing on what is happening at the present moment right on the spot.

Actually, immediacy has two meanings. The first means, "not mediated". If we restrict our discussion to this aspect, then by definition a discussion list on the net is mediated in two ways: first the contact goes through another medium (this aspect will be the same when we talk on the phone), and then the asynchrony means that time is mediating between responses (the same as in writing letters).

But immediacy is used in another meaning in group therapy. This aspect is related to the "here and now", and is mentioned by Ormont in his book *The Group Therapy Experience* (1992, p. 43) as "on-the-spot emotional experience" of oneself. If we relate to this aspect of immediacy then we can have an on-the-spot emotional experience to the writing of people on the Internet forum or Facebook and be aware of it. There might be some strong emotional responses to others' e-mails. The emotions people feel are to posts appearing days ago but they *are* "on-the-spot". (Chat rooms are closer to the immediacy response because the interaction is synchronic and concurrent.)

Although there might be a delay in reaction, the internal responses of the reader are immediate. Immediacy implies "right now", but what kind of "right now" response will be considered as immediacy? Maybe we have to define a new "immediacy" for Internet interaction? Here is what a participant in the group-psychotherapy international discussion list wrote about it which describes very well this new approach:

> If I have an immediate response to someone's post, my reaction to it is also immediate. But I have a dilemma of how to try and communicate that reaction across a medium that has no facial expression, no tone of voice, no non-verbals to speak of, emotions notwithstanding. My own approach to this is to spend some time formulating my language carefully, so as to convey my response as precisely as possible, nuanced so as to convey my "immediate" experience. Granted, this is a different way of thinking about immediacy, but it's as valid a representation of what I can come up with at the moment. (Personal communication, the group psychotherapy discussion list, 7 April 2001)

If immediacy usually means having an immediate response to the other, on Cyberspace it will become having immediate response to the other's message.

Presence as realism

In this conceptualisation presence is determined by "the degree to which a medium can produce seemingly accurate representations of objects, events and people - representations that look, sound, and/or feel like the 'real' thing" (Lombard & Ditton, 1997, p. 6). This aspect touches the old philosophical question of "what is real?" and is used as the main argument by conservatives against relationship on the Internet, "but this is not *real* relationship." But how real is real?

According to Lacan (1977) three layers construct the human experience: the real, the imaginary, and the symbolic. The symbolic realm is achieved when entering language. We encounter language from the minute we are born and given a name. The world is already structured for us through words. Human beings cannot exist outside language. Language not only represents objects but also "creates the world of objects". The imaginary is created when a child sees a reflection in the mirror and the adult says, "This is you." This way the child identifies himself erroneously with what s/he is not. The result is an ego alienated from the self. The imaginary is the total identifications of the ego and its relationship with its objects. The real relates to the human existence before entering the symbolic, the world of words. It relates to the primary unity, when we are not aware of any lack, or any differentiated objects. It is a transcendental experience.

Lacan's theory implies that most of our existence is in the symbolic realm. It is interesting to note that what Lacan labels "real" is very different from what people mean "real" in everyday life. What we consider "real" is actually symbolic and only signifies reality. This argument stresses the critical importance of reality representations, mostly language. Words only point to other signifiers and not to any entity beyond language (Barratt, 1993). Derrida (1974) connects this illusion that words represent reality to the fact that when a person speaks, his voice seems to carry the expressions of his subjectivity and mental experience. It appears as "the unique experience of the signified producing itself spontaneously from within the self'" (p. 20). Speech receives a transcendental meaning, or as Sampson (1989, p. 9) writes explaining Derrida, "a source which itself has no source other than its pure being, pure spontaneity, pure presence; a source that serves the ground for truth itself".

There are several philosophers who touch the question of reality and its representations, including Plato, who claimed that earthly-materialistic-sensual reality could only reflect the shadows and imitations of ideas (the famous cave fable), and Kant who argued that we could never grasp the "thing in itself" with our mind and senses. Among psychoanalysts Bion (1984) distinguishes between the sphere of ultimate truth, that can be known out of experience, but we can never really know about (he labelled it O), and intellectual knowledge (which he labelled K).

The important issue here is that what we consider "real" is bound to interpretations and is not necessarily what is perceived by our senses. The most common meaning of "real" is what we perceive by our sense. Can we not trust our senses at least? Actually, no. The brain only interprets the stimulus that is transmitted by the neuron and we believe it shows "the truth". In the world of virtual reality, where we can wear a helmet with virtual glasses and gloves and believe whatever illusion the computer creates, we cannot distinguish between what we imagine and what "really" exists anymore. If we wear special eyeglasses with lens that turn the world upside down, at first we shall see the world upside down, but after a few days our brain will adapt itself to the "new world" and show us "the real world".

Perhaps this is the reason why a movie such as *The Matrix* gained so much popularity after its appearance in 1999. Disguised as a science-fiction-action movie, it actually asks the question "what is real?" and offers a simplistic answer that we live in an imaginary world created by a computer program. So the world around us is just an illusion. *The Matrix* is the network designed to make us believe that the world we "see" and "sense" is the real world. In the Internet world this is actually what happens. People are connected to one another through invisible wires, relate to the environment they face as real, and belong to virtual communities in which they are emotionally invested. Maybe twenty years ago, before Cyberspace became ubiquitous, a film like *The Matrix* could not become so popular.

Presence as transportation

This definition of presence involves the idea of transportation, whether the user is transported to another place, or another place and its objects are transported to the user, or both people in interaction are transported to another place. Consider the science fiction movie *Avatar* (2009) where humans have genetically grown half-alien/half-human bodies which they can jack their consciousnesses into and explore the world. These hybrid avatars are operated by genetically matched humans who are transferred into these bodies. The presence of the movie's protagonist avatar is so real that it allows romantic relationship with the Na'vi native tribe heroine.

Transportation to another place does not necessarily have to involve a traffic vehicle. It only requires good imagination. When two lovers immerse in an intimate conversation they feel as if they are taken from the regular everyday reality and are both transferred into a world only they share. When you watch a good movie and you are totally absorbed in it, you feel as if you are transferred into another world.

The therapeutic hour transfers its two participants to another world too, protected from the regular everyday reality. Clients often complain that the therapeutic relationship is "unreal" and that they feel as if surrounded by a bubble. This bubble is necessary in order to create a safe environment, different from "reality". The therapeutic holding environment is a safe womb giving the client the feeling that s/he can talk about everything without being judged. The unconditional acceptance and positive regard of the therapist (Rogers, 1957) brings back the client to the lost Garden of Eden of childhood, whether s/he really had such an experience in the past or just longed to have one. The therapist creates this "illusionary reality" by his or her unique presence. The psychotherapist develops a special presence by giving up his needs and "ego" and being there for the client. Self-psychology describes this presence, as being ready to serve as the patient's self-object. In this position, through empathy, the therapist reaches the almost impossible achievement of "touching the subject from zero distance" (Kulka, 1991).

Analytic and therapeutic groups can create this illusion of being transferred to another place too. The group reflects the outside world on one hand, but it also creates its own culture, own norms and unique ways of behaviour. In therapy groups people can be honest and open, disclose issues they never talk about and express their feelings in an intensity they never dared to share in the "real world". Entering regression, participants unconsciously perceive the group as a mother and merging fantasies are often activated (Foguel, 1994; Scheidlinger, 1974). In fact, we can often hear people "complaining" about the warm-intimate relationship developing in these groups that they are not real, just as people complain about Internet connections.

Virtual reality strongly shakes our regular perception of "presence". In virtual reality people are transferred into an imaginary reality which imitates so well "real" reality and sometimes cannot be distinguished from it. Objects presented in virtual reality can easily be mistaken for real ones. What happens when we project a virtual therapist and conduct a therapeutic session in virtual reality? This possibility upsets the conservative norms of therapy that perceive two embodied persons in interaction as a necessary condition for therapy. We can go further and think about a group of people meeting in virtual reality for group therapy, each of them stays at home but their image is projected onto a virtual room where the group meets. There is no reason why the results of such group sessions should be different from face to face meetings as long as the illusion of reality and the sense of presence is well-kept.

Presence as immersion

This feature of presence is closely related to the idea of presence as transportation, because when we are psychologically and perceptually immersed, the body is entrusted into another reality. Actually this component stands behind imagined transportation. As described before, the presence of the therapist is one of the most important factors that determine the result of therapy. This unique presence is achieved by being genuinely involved and absorbed in the story of the client, almost "forgetting" the therapist's own interests and needs. Although, in the beginning the relationship with the therapist seems to clients artificial, they find themselves more involved in the therapeutic relationship and the presence of the therapist accompanies them in the break between the sessions. When this happens, clients find themselves "talking" to their therapist in their imagination, consulting them in their minds, and imagining their answers. The psychotherapist is becoming "a good internal object" for the client.

We can observe the same phenomenon in groups. Members who become engaged in group therapy report that they feel the group as accompanying them in their everyday life, giving them support, strength, and courage to do things they refrained from doing before. The intense relationships and interactions occurring during the group meeting have their impact and exert their influence outside the group too. If the group represents a mother figure, it is internalised as a good mother encouraging the development of her child.

Csikszentmihalyi (1990) describes a mental state in which a person is fully immersed in an activity with both involvement and focus. He calls this state "flow". When people enter this state, they concentrate on a limited field so that they feel fully present and their anxiety dissipates. This experience can happen in Cyberspace and online forums.

Presence as immersion is the most obvious feature of romantic relationship on the Internet. The lovers are involved in an intense bond even though they might have never met one another face to face. They perceive their relationship as real, bringing happiness to their lives and influencing their day-to-day routine more than many other persons they meet. When someone is involved with a lover overseas, others might call him a virtual object, but looking deeper into love relationship with its typical idealisation, lovers relate to one another in an unrealistic way, projecting their ego-ideal onto one another and creating virtual objects even when they meet daily.

Psychologically, one can say that *every internal object is a virtual object*. Internal objects have no body, no concrete contour features. They are representations of real objects for sure, but they do not represent these objects with ingenuous realistic details. The psychoanalytic school of object relations is based on the hypothesis that we internalise the significant others from birth on as internal representations and their inner relations guide our lives. Dismissing virtual objects as unreal and unimportant means dismissing the object relations approach in psychotherapy and denying the fact that our personality is composed of virtual (internalised) objects.

Presence as social actor within medium and presence as medium as social actor

These two characteristics of presence are intertwined and cannot be discussed separately. One deals with relating to a person or computer character and the other deals with relating to cues provided by the medium itself. When interacting with a social actor within a medium, such as a TV broadcaster or computer software imitating a person, people tend to disregard the one-sided interaction, and forget how mediated and artificial this relationship is. A cyber pet, such as "the Tamagotchi" can acquire features of, and children might treat it as, a "real" pet.

The famous ELIZA software from 1966 imitating a therapeutic session gave the impression of an empathic and accepting Rogerian psychologist. The possibility of a Cyber-psychologist brings to mind the old debate about "Turing Test", and whether a computer can completely mimic a human being. In this test (named after Alan Turing who first suggested it) a person should try to differentiate between two actors, leading a conversation with the person behind a screen, and decide which of them is flesh and blood and which is a machine. Many science-fiction movies focus on such a possibility, sometimes evoking archaic fears about machines controlling humans (*Space Odyssey 2001*, *The Matrix*, etc.) and sometimes arousing social and ethical questions (*Artificial Intelligence*, *Blade Runner*, etc.). In the Internet era one can never know whether the person with whom we are connected on-line is a "real" person or just a sophisticated computer programme.

Considering the above, there is no reason to think that a Cyber-psychologist (a machine that imitates the professional responses of a psychologist) will have a different impact on the client than a real therapist. As long as the illusion of presence is working, and the social cues that are normally reserved for human-to-human interaction exist in this interaction, we can perceive the entity on the other end as a real social entity and relate to him as such.

An Internet group example

Although the role of the group leader on the Internet will be discussed in detail in Chapter Five, including the importance of his/her presence, the following example brings to the fore some questions about the way his/her authority might be present and how different cultures interpret it. Before bringing the example, let me remind you that different cultures create different frames of references for group therapy. These differences are reflected even in the name of the group therapist, which is called group leader in the USA and group conductor in the UK. This is not just a semantic question, as we know that language shapes our mind. A leader has the authority to make decisions and to lead the group in the way s/he finds right. A conductor tries to integrate between the different voices and in group analysis s/he becomes a more equal partner of the group. The seemingly slight differences become prominent in the following example taken from my group-psychotherapy Internet discussion list (this discussion list will be described in Chapter Six):

> A stormy exchange of e-mails took over the scene on the list when a new member entered the discussion. She was definitely not a group therapist like the other participants, and had a lot of criticism towards therapists, which she aimed towards the list members. At the same time she sent so many messages that the members were overwhelmed with the volume of e-mails. Some of them attacked her and some tried to protect and understand her. After some interpretative intervention, in an effort to quiet the scene, the list manager (myself) decided to take a "leader's" stance and announced that this member's (S.) posts will be reviewed by him prior to releasing them to the list. In addition he restricted her postings to five a day.

> A very hot discussion followed his decisions. Here are some responses:

>> Thank you Haim. For me this quiets down the voice inside that has been telling me to leave the list. The past events on the list have made it hard to simply lurk and remain on the sidelines due to the huge amounts of maintenance required just to keep my inbox from being overrun with group psychotherapy messages. I think your strategy is a good one.

>> Throughout the tumult that has occurred over the last several days, when the topic of what to do or what not to do about S.'s behaviour arose there was usually a comparison made to a therapy group. I'd like to propose a different analogy. I agree with A. when he said "I have found the forum to be an oasis in my life as a place to come and share ideas, make friends both professionally and personally, and once and a while laugh." With that in mind I prefer to liken this forum to a professional meeting or workshop. If someone claiming to be a member of our profession entered our meeting and behaved in the way that S. did . . . disrupting, manic, borderline rage, etc.. . . . I know I would not turn my attention from the gathering and try to therapize (another word from the dictionary according to J.) or educate that person. I would be looking toward the people in charge to kindly escort that person out of the room and set some boundaries and limits. Giving them the choice

to participate in a way that is not destructive either to the gather-
ing or to themselves.

I think that is what Haim did . . . I am suspecting, or rather
hoping, that the five post limit will be rescinded at some point
soon, but I see it, as a necessary frame tightening for the moment.
Oh gosh . . . I think I just fell back into the therapy analogy. Lol.

So far, the messages support the leader's intervention. A hidden tacit
assumption is included in these responses, which is that the task of the
person in charge (the list manager in that case) is to set up the boundaries
and put limits to a deviating member. As pointed out before, this assumption might be part of the "taken-for-granted way" that leaders are
supposed to act in the culture of messages' writers. The writers are probably unaware that their expectations are part of a specific cultural norm.
Behind this norm many other cultural codes are concealed, such as a
patronising approach that gives leaders the authority to decide who is
behaving well and who should be restrained.

Compare these responses with another message:

I am opposed to your changes; they make me feel like giving up.

How will your changes affect other members, who have often
posted more than five times in a day? Why should you be the one
to decide which of S.'s messages is worthy of response; if she
sends sixteen will you decide which five to forward?

Part of the problem, recently has been the inability of other
members to make enlightened judgments about when and how to
respond; now you seem to be offering to do this on everyone's
behalf. I experience it as debilitating and undermining of the
group members' capacity to think about what has been troubling
them/us.

Doubtless there is great pressure on you to act in this sort of way.
Perhaps this is the "American way"—using power to step in and
solve others' problems for them.

I am fulminating.

These messages represent two ways of looking at the list manager's
actions: One is focusing on the protective function (creating a safe
environment) and the other is a developing function (giving the
opportunity for group members to solve their problems alone). Both
are valid and acceptable in various group situations. The interesting

point was that most of the list members who supported the list moderator's managerial decisions were North Americans while most of those who opposed his authoritarian position were British or Europeans. This observation leads to the assumption that the different responses represent more than individual differences and reflect deeper cultural aspects. One of the most important social institutes is the leadership unit. The different attitudes towards leadership in every culture and the diversity of interpretation of its tasks and functions in society reveal much about the elusive nature of that culture. North Americans are probably unaware how and why they are perceived as "using power to step in and solve others' problems". It is also important to note that this entire debate took place after the second Gulf War where the US decided to attack Iraq despite the world protest.

Another difference that is reflected through these responses and that might be attributed to cultural influences on group therapy is the individual point of view *vs*. the group-as-a-whole perspective. North Americans are more used to looking at the individual's welfare and achievements and focus on the person in groups too, while Europeans adopt a more systemic point of view. Individualism is a very deep value in the American tradition and myth, from the days of conquering the West. The example above leads to the conclusion that different group psychotherapy approaches that developed in various parts of the world are deeply connected to culture too. The group analytic approach, that focuses on society and sees individual and culture as interrelated and inseparable (as mentioned in Chapter Two on the group analytic frame of reference), could not easily be accepted in the American individualistic culture, but flourished well in Britain with its tradition of social parties and theories.

This example strongly relates to the question of the Internet culture as a unity mentioned in the previous chapter. We can see that although the group-psychotherapy forum members belong to the same Internet community with which they develop strong ties (and with one another), they still hold to their original values and beliefs from their "mother culture" as country or professional training. Should we give up the notion of the Internet as a holding environment new culture? Not so quickly. In one of my articles (Weinberg, 2002) I explore the common beliefs of the group psychotherapy discussion list and show the hidden values of the group therapist community. The fact that the members continue to belong to this Cyber community, and make an effort to discuss their different perspectives, means that they feel committed to dialogue around the different cultures they come from. This means that the hidden norm of this community is dialogue, not as a means to persuade the other but to be able to present your beliefs and let the other do the same with a feeling of mutual respect.

Summary

Taking into consideration all the facets of presence mentioned above we can summarize that the meaning of presence is closely related to our understanding and perceiving of reality. In the post-modern era reality cannot be described as "what is perceived by our senses". Reality is socially constructed and is based more on a consensus agreed upon in a specific society. As Mantovani & Riva put it " 'reality' is not out there in the world, somewhere 'outside' people's minds, escaping social negotiation and cultural mediation; reality is co-constructed in the relationship between actors and their environments through the mediation of the artifacts" (1999, p. 541) and "Individuals experience 'reality' through interpretive grids that are generated by the preexisting social structures that have presided over their socialization processes and live in 'reality' that is usually a social space" (1999, p. 545).

Reality is not something objective, but is constructed in people's minds according to their cultural and environmental influences, to which many of them are unconscious or at least unaware of. If we want to more deeply understand the meaning of presence and reality, we need to deconstruct these conceptions and analyse how they change according to different ontologies, in different societies and different cultures. We also need to understand the concept of the social unconscious, which is closely connected to constructing reality in society. Regarding reality as socially constructed brings forth language as the primary societal tool in constructing reality. Language not only defines objects, calls them by names, and describes them, but also moulds and shapes how we perceive the world (Derrida, 1974; Lacan, 1977).

Another conclusion is that there are no unmediated objects and unmediated communication. *All interaction is mediated, but some forms of mediation are naturalised within dominant culture.* We can start with

Derrida's (1974) argument that speech is already inhabited by writing and hence is mediated and derivative. We can also say that there is no interaction outside a medium, but the medium can appear to be transparent, and as such invisible. But above all, if reality and presence are socially constructed it means that society and culture covertly and unconsciously mediate every interaction. It is like water to fish: fish do not know that they are surrounded by water. The illusion of non-mediation might become stronger in a specific culture, reinforcing the medium to cause psychological immersion, but culture still mediates any experience of presence.

The implications of these conclusions to therapy are unperceivable. They challenge the norms common to Western society that therapy should be conducted between two embodied people (or a group of people), who are physically present having a face-to-face interaction.

Maybe we can adopt a new definition of therapy that involves two *selves* (or a group of selves) in interaction instead of two embodied persons. The self is not equivalent to the body, is not contained by the body and even does not necessarily reside inside a body. "A body is not 'covered' by the skin, it does not 'contain' the 'self'." (Correa De Jesus, 1999, p. 83). The new approach to therapy, enhanced by a new understanding of human connection appearing on-line, portrays two decentred selves, partial, subjective, and polymorphous as they are trying to connect over a mediated space, having rare moments of close-touching connection.

CHAPTER FIVE

Boundaries, boundaries, boundaries (and the forum manager/group leader's role)

Introduction: boundaries and systems

Open any textbook about groups and you will find at least one paragraph about the importance of boundaries for the development of a healthy group. In fact, boundaries are important for the development and functioning of any human system, including the individual, the family, and social groups. Mahler's (Mahler, Pine, & Bergman, 1975) developmental theory, describing how a human infant moves from symbiosis to object constancy and focusing on separation-individuation, is actually a description of the infant's struggle to develop normal boundaries which will be crucial to his/her future relationship. Although Daniel Stern (1985) proposed that an infant develops in a series of overlapping and interdependent stages or layers, which are increasingly interpersonally sophisticated, thus showing infant awareness of self/other from the beginning, Mahler's basic idea of developing boundaries is still important. Minuchin's (1974) structural approach to family therapy emphasises the importance of flexible boundaries between the family and its environment, and among sub-systems in the family (such as parents and children), focusing on the polarities of enmeshment (blurred boundaries) *vs.* disengagement (rigid boundaries). In the field of group therapy, the system centred therapy (SCT) model, developed by Agazarian (1997), described the main task of the group leader as increasing communication across boundaries, working on establishing functional subgroups and helping them explore similarities and differences.

Healthy boundaries for a living human system must be flexible enough to allow the flow of information and communication between the system and its environment. When too flexible, loose, and blurred boundaries are created, they make it difficult to distinguish what is inside the system and what is outside. Neither are too rigid boundaries desired, as this will create an encapsulated system that cannot exchange information with the outside world and becomes entrapped in its conservative patterns and myths (like China before it opened to connecting with the West). Certain personality disorders (such as borderline type) result in (or from) too blurred boundaries, while other disorders (like obsessive-compulsive) are associated with too rigid boundaries. As mentioned before, dysfunctional families either have enmeshed or detached structures, both resulting from unsuitable boundaries.

Boundaries in groups

Keeping the group setting and boundaries in small groups is important to ensure group safety and stability. The most common boundaries managed by the group leader in groups are the time and space ones. For a therapy group to function well, for members to feel safe and to allow for a facilitating environment, the starting and ending time of a session should be clear. In fact, without clear time boundaries of the session we lose our ability to interpret deviations from these boundaries. The same rule goes for the length and duration of the entire group from its conception to its well-known in advance "death" (in a time-limited group). Keeping time boundaries of the number of sessions allows us to interpret difficulties in termination, many times related to issues of loss and fear of death. The location and space of the group should also be well-defined by the environmental physical boundaries. It is important to have a constant room for a group, like a tent established every week distinguishing the group's space from its surrounding and separating daily routine and progression from the occurrences in the group.

Boundaries are especially important for enhancing self-disclosure in groups. The question of confidentiality, or what information is kept only inside the group, provides another example of a boundary issue. It is one of the conductor's tasks to protect the boundaries of the group, although it is not always clear when s/he should take practical steps or just interpret the boundary violation in order to restore safety.

The boundaries of the self system should also be considered when talking about groups. Participants need to feel that they have control of the amount of exposure and the personal information they share. Thus, pressure on group members to reveal secrets or share more than they want, is harmful. This pressure, by the way, might not be so direct and visible, so it is the role of the leader to pay attention and encourage this regulation of self-boundaries in the group. Sometimes the group conductor has to check if a group member's boundaries were not violated without noticing. At times, I have chosen to intervene, stopping a member from sharing too much simply by asking them whether they really want to go further exploring an issue or are they unconsciously yielding to other people's expectations. Self-boundaries can be well preserved in a small group as most people can easily control their level of self-disclosure. Self-boundaries are different in a large group. Although on the one hand, overt group pressures on the individual are less common, there are hidden unconscious pressures creating situations where members of the large group speak against their decision to stay quiet. Members of the large group can feel sucked into a role and find themselves representing positions they never thought they would express.

Boundaries and culture

Western cultures are so used to taking boundaries seriously, and perceiving boundary keeping (especially of meeting times) as crucial for obtaining adult responsibilities and business obligations, that it is hard to imagine that different cultures relate very differently to the issue of boundaries. In fact, when a Northern American person schedules a business meeting with someone from Latin America who is late for the meeting, it is difficult for the person who is accustomed to Western norms not to interpret this lateness of the Latin American as rude, irresponsible, or disrespectful. A cultural lens reveals a very different perspective: attitudes towards time boundaries in South America (and some other non-Western parts of the world) can be very lenient, and it is not realistic to expect people from the Mediterranean to be strictly on time in the way people are used to in Northern Europe.

Beyond misunderstandings and confusions around business meetings or multicultural encounters, these differences pose a question for the group theoretician. If group boundaries are so important and essential in creating a safe environment, how can groups in those parts of the world who do not strictly attend to boundaries become efficient and successful? What allows these groups to be therapeutic? Do people in Latin America need less safety? Because group psychotherapy literature emphasises boundaries so much, non-Western/Northern hemisphere groups seem to contradict some very basic rules common to all groups.

Although the need for boundaries seems universal, and it often goes without saying that the sense of security in a group depends on keeping a strict setting, the amount of boundaries needed for self-security is culturally based. Cultures differ significantly in their members' need to guard their privacy. This difference in boundary keeping is manifested not only in the different body proximity kept in an encounter in various societies, but also in the depth of personal information a person is ready to share with other members of his community.

In a professional visit to Brazil (August 2004) I was invited to one of the poor neighbourhoods (a *favela*) to observe a session of "community therapy" that took place in one of the huts of the community centre. The event takes place once a week, and participation is allowed for anyone interested. About thirty people were present in the meeting we attended, most of them *favela* inhabitants. I was surprised at the level of personal problems presented. I thought that in community therapy people would talk about problems of the community, but they presented the same problems I am used to in my therapy groups. A woman told about her daughter who had a relationship with a married man. When the daughter decided to leave him, this man became aggressive and broke the furniture in their house. One day he drugged the mother and she found herself with him naked in bed. Another person presented himself as a physician who works in the community and was told to stop working for the poor. The third speaker had learning difficulties and said that only half of his brain functions. His friend came with him to help him in case he forgot to say something important.

Later, I asked the interpreters how these people could talk about such intimate issues in public. They told us that poor people have nothing to lose, and that in these poor neighbourhoods, everyone knows what's going on in his neighbour's bedroom. Many issues of boundaries and confidentiality in that "community therapy" session were very different from what I am used to in my practice. People went in and out, children were there (sometimes trying to sell us post-cards), the whole event was recorded (probably for research purposes, but as far as I noticed without asking the people's permission), and during the session hostesses entered with some food and a drink. Still it seems that the participants were not troubled by the boundary violation. On the other hand, we cannot ignore the role of the inter-preters in structuring the account I conceptualised, and perhaps the poor people did object, or maybe they are accustomed to being treated with disrespect.

It seems that even though boundaries are not strictly kept in non-Northern Hemisphere countries, group therapy there is as effective as we know it in the West, and the contents of sessions are similar. We might say that when cultural norms do not demand strict boundaries, people's expectations are different regarding what creates safety in the group. But certainly there must be something else that provides this safety, otherwise it is hard to imagine what facilitates the trust needed to share intimate details. What is that factor that provides safety?

Let us leave this question open for a while and focus on another kind of group whose boundaries are loose: the large group.

Boundaries in the large group

As a reminder, when I talk about the large group in the context of this book, I relate to the kind of a group we see more and more in confer-ences, especially group psychotherapy ones (at the American Group

Psychotherapy Association—AGPA, the International Group Analytic Society—GASi, the International Association of Group Psychotherapy—IAGP) and also in conferences focusing on exploring authority and leadership issues (human relations conferences, such as Leicester in the UK/Europe and A. K. Rice Institute in the USA), or focusing on social issues (exploring relationship between social groups in conflict).

The large group is a group of more than twenty-five to thirty-five people conducted psychodynamically. Its dynamics are different from those typical of the small group (Weinberg & Schneider, 2003) in many ways. For example, in a large group you cannot expect the same level of intimacy people are used to in the small therapy group. Members who join the large group with an expectation for such an intimate experience, are strongly disappointed. Usually, large groups do not focus on individuals but on group-as-a-whole processes, learning from the here-and-now about organisational or societal processes and especially about the social unconscious (Hopper & Weinberg, 2011).

What was written above about boundaries cannot be attained in large groups. The boundaries of these groups are too flexible and fluid to strictly be kept. In short, the large group is a weakened container. In a large group people can come to, or be absent from a meeting without anyone noticing them. When there are hundreds of members in the group, no one notices if someone does not come to a specific session, or enters as a newcomer in the second session. It is not the spatial concrete boundaries that determine who belongs to the large group and who is excluded. What determines a sense of inclusion and belonging is not clear-cut boundaries. We can relate to large groups as representing organisations, ethnic groups, or society-at-large. Thus, I can leave my country to live in another place, and still feel like an Israeli, behave like an Israeli and be considered an Israeli by others. Participating in a large group is more like belonging to a community. The level of involvement and commitment of the participants signifies their being part of their community.

Even self-boundaries might not be kept well in a large group. First, a member can disappear in the crowd and merge with the herd. Turquet (1975) talks about threats to identity in the large group. The individual might feel like a cog in the machine. Even finding one's voice in the crowd can be difficult, and for some people just expressing their thoughts in the large group feels like an achievement. Participants in large groups often feel as if they are "suffering from a fracture of their personality" (Anzieu, 1984, p. 80). Hopper's (2009) innovative perception of the life of social systems is relevant here and is strongly activated in large groups: as mentioned in Chapter Two, he presented the fourth basic assumption expressed in bi-polar forms of *incohesion: aggregation/massification or (ba) I:AM*. When this assumption is activated (as it is in the large group), groups and group-like social systems oscillate between aggregation and massification.

Experiences from either participating in or leading large groups showed me that although their boundaries are looser than those created and maintained in small therapy groups, there is still a level of belonging and involvement in their sessions. More than that, when a large group has enough time to develop and enter advanced stages, sometimes surprisingly intimate moments occur among the crowd. Members shift from an isolated self, to becoming intersubjectively inter-related and move towards mutual recognition.

Here is a vignette from a large group in this stage of development:

> In a two day large group in an international preconference taking place in a European country, during the first day the group was quiet for a long time, and seemed heavy and stuck. People were not able to speak freely, many of them were silent and even when they spoke it seemed as if they spoke to themselves with only a few interactions and responses following. The efforts of the large group leaders to interpret the obstacles, talk about the anxiety, fear of judgment, and difficulty with languages did not help a lot easing the process. Issues relating to threat of erasing the identity of the country hosting the conference, leaving its members powerless, surfaced, but could not be expressed directly or thoroughly discussed. Immigration appeared to be one theme that was related to this issue.

> At the beginning of the second day, one of the leaders summarised all the possible difficulties that prevented people from talking and empathised with the difficulty of the task: to be open in a large multi-lingual, multi-cultural group. People kept coming late to the group and a member expressed her annoyance with that boundary violation. One of the leaders said that the group reminded him of more and more immigrants coming to a country. Following this opening, one of the members brought a dream where he owned a shop in a street, among many other shops. Chinese people started buying all the shops around his shop until he had no other way but sell his shop too, with a great loss of money. The group

had many associations and responses to this dream. One member noticed that there are no Chinese in the group and one of the leaders joked that, even in his dream, his unconscious made an effort not to insult anyone.

In this stage, members of the large groups communicate better, listen to one another and are able to respect more their differences. Some amount of cohesion seems to be achieved so that the loose boundaries have been transformed into imaginary established boundaries. Particularly, what allows the possibility of mutual recognition? How do these groups overcome their problematic boundaries and create enough safety to allow for the vulnerability accompanying more personal intersubjective interactions? Is it just a matter of time, or does the leader have a part in helping the large group reach these achievements? In my opinion it is not enough that the leader will allow it to happen by not interrupting the process, but s/he must also be active in interpreting the difficulty of accepting the other and recognising subjective experiences as valid. The leader's function and active presence in emphasising mutual recognition is crucial in compensating for the loose boundaries. In order to reach mutual acknowledgement and acceptance, the focus should be on intersubjective matters and the approach of the group leaders should be relational.

Boundaries on the Internet

Boundaries in Internet groups seem non-existent. There are neither spatial boundaries, as Cyberspace is endless, nor time boundaries, as the Internet forum never stops and people can write to it all the time. However, self boundaries can be well preserved. People can at least keep the illusion of having control over what they write. It is interesting to notice that under such conditions of anonymity, people tend to reveal more than in a face-to-face meeting. According to any theory of group therapy and group processes, the lack of clear boundaries on the Internet should restrict the possibility of group cohesion, reduce the sense of safety, and limit intimate talk. However, as mentioned in the previous chapter, self-disclosure is surprisingly high despite loose boundaries and a flexible setting in the Internet forum and online discussion lists. McKenna, Green, and Gleason (2002) explained this phenomenon as due to the anonymity of the members in these forums, which reduces the risks of ridicule or rejection of people disclosing personal information, and compared it to the "stranger in the train" phenomenon. My observation is that it also happens in forums where members do not disguise their identity and are not anonymous. One possible explanation for this surprising self-disclosure is creation and development of a core group (see Chapter Six) that demonstrates group norms of tolerance and openness, and develops an atmosphere of cohesion, "we-ness", and belonging. The core group helps developing the illusion of a small group in a large group setting. The core group consists of members that are more involved in the exchange of messages, post more often and become more salient and important in this large group. At times, this core group looks as a closed group with its own boundaries, including only certain members, and at first this perception might restrict the participation of new members. However, once the newcomer is ready to respect the group norms and its veterans, and is ready to take the risks and send more messages, he or she can be included in that core group. New people who join the group later cannot differentiate between active-involved members who joined the group a few months ago, and those who were there from the beginning.

In addition, members writing on the Internet feel control over their self-boundaries. Sitting in a private room, without seeing the others or being seen by them and being dressed informally (or hardly at all), gives a sense of protection and of more control over the amount of disclosure. Because the writer feels there is more choice about what to reveal, s/he is able to write many personal things, especially if the general atmosphere of the group is accepting and tolerant. Another aspect that contributes to this disclosure, and that will be discussed later in detail, is the presence of the forum's leader.

Although Internet forums and the Brazilian *favela* population (whose community therapy groups were described above) seem to be very different communities—one associated with rich countries and financially secure people and the other associated with very poor people—they both point out the same issue around self-disclosure: Safety is not so dependent on concrete-physical boundaries as we are used to thinking in the Western world. A sense of belonging to a community is not determined by its spatial location, and the group ego-skin (to use Anzieu's (1999) wonderful term) provides a sense of safety under an illusionary virtual envelope that can be expanded to include communities, large groups, ethnic groups, nations, etc.

Here is an e-mail sent to the group psychotherapy list, summarising well, both the core group and the large group phenomena, and portraying the ability to be open and involved despite the obstacles (Personal communication, group psychotherapy discussion list, 13 May 1998):

> Hello Forum Members,
>
> I've been watching the heated discussions on several topics for some time, have been tempted and resisted all together to jump into the subjects, feeling resistance for a few reasons:
>
> 1) I agree with P.'s fishbowl metaphor that the discussions round up between a certain number of members. When I enter into my email account and start watching the incoming mails, I can almost guess which names will appear. And I make interior comments such as : "Oh wow, what happened to S., G., K, C. et al. that they're not responding this time?"??? Maybe some overdoers jumping immediately into each subject are inhibiting other members and not allowing enough space, thus indirectly creating underdoers?
>
> This is definitely an observation and a trial to understand the process, definitely not an indirect way of trying to stop ANYONE. I personally enjoy a lot the heated responses of some members and have already formed certain first impressions figures which amuses me beforehand when I think to compare them with the 'real person', time coming i.e. next AGPA conference??? Therefore, S., G., K., C. et al. please keep posting.
>
> 2) I realize that the "fishbowl" is made of mostly USA, which means that some jokes, references, etc. are not familiar to me, which means that sometimes the forum discussions take a language that might be foreign to some of us, i.e. to me.
>
> 3) As a woman, I don't feel intimidated at all, neither resistant to the computer or to email correspondence. Nowadays I don't see computer resistance as a gender issue anymore. I think that gender differences come more with what M. mentions:
>
> Some of us are more tuned to faces than others. I am much less articulate on the phone unless I know the person well. So it takes me longer on the list to feel connected (maybe this is a female thing?)
>
> Does this attitude come from female sensitivity to others' reactions or a still carried and disguised way of seeking approval for what we say???

4) Some resistance and intimidation might come from non-response. I personally have experienced that for the very few postings I've made, i.e. presenting myself, etc. non-response made me feel like saying "hello" from the top of a mountain into a void, without any echo: weird, lonely, unheard, non-acknow-ledged, discouraged. Watching the forum discussions, to my observation, some members get response for anything they say, and some are let down. (This certainly is not my feeling, I don't feel let down, since I'm not REALLY trying to get in mostly by choice, for the reason underneath:

5) My real resistance comes more from a choice. After long hours of therapy, I sometimes want to switch off into something differ-ent: music, reading, talking to a friend, etc. I feel myself resistant to sit in front of the computer which I consider as 'work'. Therefore, jumping into the subject is taking responsibility—response-ability.

Then, why did I change my attitude this time? Because, P., S., K., M., N. and F.'s postings seemed very inviting, genuinely concerned with the process and I thought it would be quite unfair to sit and watch without taking charge this time.

Part-time lurker willing to step out.

As seen in the next chapter, periods of intimate talk and emotional tone similar to those occurring in a small group (see discussion under "Or is it a small group?" Chapter Six), can be achieved in a virtual group as well. People are ready to self-disclose personal events and feelings (in self-help groups for traumatised people, members may reveal secrets they never told anybody) not only under the conditions of anonymity, and members ignore the lack of boundaries and the flawed container. Is it possible that these are signs of a new culture where self-boundaries are lenient and privacy becomes old-fash-ioned? Can we conclude that this Internet "brave new world" diffuses boundaries not only between countries and cultures, but also blurs self boundaries, ultimately creating a mass of Internet "we-ness" (Lawrence, Bain, & Gould, 1996)?

Boundaries and the role of the group leader/moderator

Group therapists who moderate online *listserves* relate to Internet forums in one of the following ways:

1. Seeing it as a way to express their thoughts, exchange ideas and connect with colleagues, hence denying its similarity to a group, and managing it technically.
2. Understanding that an Internet forum is a group, focusing more on its similarity to face-to-face groups. When they do relate to Internet forums as a group, some group therapists see it more as a small group, while others understand that it also has large group qualities.
3. Understanding that an Internet forum is a group, different from face-to-face in some ways.

In the introduction of this book, I described how I developed and changed my ideas about Internet groups and the way to conduct them, focusing at first on their similarities to a small group. Later, understanding how different an Internet forum is from a small face-to-face group and how it resembles a large group. Still recently, seeing more and more features typical of Internet groups that are different from any face-to-face groups.

In the absence of clear boundaries of Internet forums pointed out above (both spatial and time boundaries), some other factor should compensate for this lack in order to make it a more holding environment (Winnicott, 1986) and restore the containing function of this leaking container. The role of the leader of Internet groups is crucial in creating relative safety under these conditions. The leader (sometimes called moderator in Cyberspace although it does not necessarily mean that s/he moderates the forum by censoring certain e-mails) can influence the psychological climate in Internet groups by executing well the administrative function, and by specific interventions derived from group therapy and group analytic tradition.

The administrative function of the group conductor is far beyond a technical issue, and relates to many psychodynamic undercurrent issues. For example, in a face-to-face group, if the group conductor arranges the chairs for the group in a circle, this closed form with its ancient associations of a womb conveys the meaning of a perfect maternal container. The conductor takes charge of the administration of the group's setting and translates "external material" brought within these boundaries, where appropriate, as matter pertaining to the dynamic flow of communication "here and now". This is why Foulkes (1975) calls this task, which includes attending to events at and beyond the boundaries of the group, ever in the service of the group's better understanding of its experience, "dynamic administration".

Holding is the main function of the leader in the "virtual" large group. In a boundless "virtual" large group, the administrative function of the leader is crucial for creating a holding environment. In small face-to-face groups the holding function is similar to the work of the blue-collar worker. The leader provides the basic conditions for making the environment convenient. The group members should be free of worries about the physical environment in order to be able to work on their psychological issues. How does the group leader achieve this function on the Internet? In the simplest form, holding occurs by being available to quickly respond to technical questions and solving technological difficulties. We need to remember that many adults participating in virtual communication still feel anxious when they enter this unknown country and behave like immigrants who do not know the norms and language, who depend on their children's competence and skills navigating in this scary land. The forum leader does not have to be an expert in technology in order to be helpful. It is enough that s/he knows how to subscribe and unsubscribe members and direct the more complicated questions to the IT people.

In addition to maintaining the dynamic administration of the forum, the leader is able to influence the atmosphere of the group and increase the feeling of safety of its members by the way s/he intervenes. Yalom and Leszcz (2005) describe the group therapist as establishing and building the group culture. The therapist shapes the group norms, such as enhancing interaction among the members and not just with the leader, directly and indirectly. Group leaders can use direct instructions, social reinforcement, or operant techniques to shape the group behaviour. They also set the example for group members by their personal behaviour in the group, most often utilising modelling.

By the same token, the leader/moderator of the virtual group is able to shape and impact the culture of these forums. They are able to do that even by procedural decisions. For example, in the Internet forum of the Group Analytic Society (GASi), the moderator announced that he was going to let the members know when someone signed off the list. Usually the Internet group members are unaware when someone unsubscribed (which is one aspect of this faceless, boundless group). This decision seems to be a procedural one, but it clearly belongs to the dynamic administration aspect and has deep dynamic meaning: The forum leader is trying to make the virtual group more similar to a face-to-face group, to increase the contact among members and to reduce the anonymity of Cyberspace.

The presence of forum leaders should be felt beyond their administrative functioning. As we discussed the concept of "presence" in Chapter Four, it does not necessitate a body. The presence of the group leader in Internet forums is felt through his or her responsiveness. First, s/he is there to help people with technicalities, but beyond that (following one of the aspects of presence discussed), s/he transmits social richness through warmth, sensitivity, and being personal when interacting with other people on the Internet. This is not an easy task to achieve, and it is hardly surprising that many Internet forums do not develop into more intimate stages. I might even say that the atmosphere on Internet groups and forums is highly determined by the attitude of the group leaders, their involvement, how immersed they are in this job, and how warmly they respond to forum members. Unfortunately, because most Internet forum leaders do this job voluntarily, in their (highly limited) free time, and as most of them do not see these forums as groups (and even if they do, they lack the group therapists' skills or Internet group leaders' training), most of the Internet lists are only used for the practical exchange of information and do not develop beyond the first stage in groups.

Most of the forums on the Internet are not process groups. They focus on a subject that interests its members and is specified in the forum title (e.g., parenting, French films, addictions, etc.). What does this imply about the leader's interventions and especially to the use of interpretations? In task (content-process) groups, the leader should interpret the process only when a serious interruption erupts, blocking the group from working on its task. As long as the working group prevails there is no need for interpretation. The same applies to the large group on the Internet. There is no need for the leader to interpret the process, unless some crisis occurs or the group is severely distracted from achieving its goals. For example, when the group faces a danger of turning a member into a scapegoat, a leader intervention is necessary, preferably by an interpretation first, or with a question that contains interpretive potentials.

The boundless world and the transference towards the leader

Immigrating into Cyberspace and entering the world of Internet forums, even mature adults feel insecure and in need of guidance. The Internet regression (Holland, 1996) impacts the attitude towards the group moderator, who is perceived as wise, benevolent, and powerful. Actually, it enhances Bion's dependency basic assumption (1959) to govern the scene in an Internet forum. Contrary to what happens in face-to-face large groups, the main transference towards the leader identified in the large group in the virtual environment, at least for some time, is idealisation. This phenomenon does not subside even after a long period of existence of the group. This phenomenon is in sharp contrast to Anzieu (1984) who argues that the collective transference generally appears as negative transference in non-directive large groups.

The lack of cues, other than textual ones on the Internet, can lead to two different options. One is the projection of aggressive feelings and interpreting ambiguities in a negative way. This was described earlier as leading to the sudden, intensive development of "flame wars". Another possibility is that people tend to "fill in the blanks" with idealisation instead of suspicion. Internet group members project the qualities of the good-enough conductor and idealise the function of the manager because they need a safe object in this vast anxiety-provoking environment. All the conductor has to do is to provide the participants with adequate holding in order to maintain this idealisation for a long time.

The Internet group leader holds a lot of power, because in theory s/he can easily censor participants and block their ability to send messages to the forum. Contrary to face-to-face groups, the leader in Cyberspace can do it without anyone noticing it (and if somehow it is revealed, s/he can always blame technology). Several times when members of my group psychotherapy list became very critical of my interventions (usually in times of crisis when they needed me to be more present and were disappointed with my inability "to save" the forum from turmoil and intense conflict), I fantasised about using my power to block these responses. I assume that my experience as a group therapist who is used to working through countertransference responses and self-analysing my own motives helped me avoid these tyrannical responses. This is why it is so important to encourage the emergence of a defiant leader (as will be mentioned in the next chapter) who warns the group about the power of the leader and the merging tendencies.

Idealisation of the Internet large group leader is enhanced by virtue of this media. When the participants are not very computer-sophisticated (and most mental health professionals are computer beginners or even computer-illiterate, especially when they are not young therapists) they start their Internet discussion list experience with some inferiority feelings and anxiety evoked by the unknown situation. As a result, they easily project wisdom and computer-wizardry onto the leader. In asynchronic discussion lists based on e-mail communication (as opposed to synchronic chat rooms, in which the participants in a discussion are present at the same time), the list leader has enough time to consider responses and not act them out even when the list is very stormy. In face-to-face groups, the group exerts a lot of pressure on the group leader to intervene when the process seems to get out of control. It is difficult for the leader to stay in an observing mode and plan the intervention calmly when regressive dynamics take over and the group uses projective identification mechanisms, pushing the leader to action. On the Internet, in the absence of time pressures, the virtual large group leader can even consult a colleague when a difficult situation arises, before intervening. This makes the leader's intervention more optimal and adds to the idealisation of the leader.

Unfortunately, idealisation is a double edged sword. It fosters unrealistic expectations of the group leader and, when these expectations are not met, the group becomes furious. For example, on one forum the members changed from admiring the leader to being very disappointed and turning against her when they found out that one of the members of the forum was an imposter and made up a false crisis in his life. They were angry that the group leader did not detect that this member was an imposter beforehand.

Winnicott (1958) traces the development of the capacity of the individual to be alone, paradoxically, as quite compatible with the other's presence. He describes a sequence of relationship around playing, starting from merging between the baby and the object, then gaining more confidence with the mother whom the baby can find (thus giving the baby some experience of magical control and omnipotence). The next stage is the capacity to be alone in the presence of the other. The child is now playing on the basis of the assumption that the mother is reliable and available.

We can say that in order to play (=be) alone, the person needs to internalise the presence of the (m)other. However, only mastering a break in this continuum makes it possible for "bodily needs" to be transformed into "ego needs". To be able to tell oneself "I am alone" without feeling forsaken means to be assured of a sense of continuity between oneself and the other person. According to Winnicott, imaginary working out of physical experience allows for a psychological capacity to be born.

Does this process remind you of what happens online? Carla Penna (personal communication, group psychotherapy discussion list, 17 January 2013) suggested that Winnicott's ideas described above explain some of our experience on an online forum, and I embrace her suggestion. Indeed, this process suits the internet well. In different parts of the world and different time zones we can have the real illusion that we are talking face-to-face in a concrete group. The group exists and does not exist at the same time. This ability to play with the other forum members, keeping their virtual presence in our mind, develops through mental practice, transforming the physical embodied group into an imagined virtual internalised group. It happens first through the presence of the forum leader described in the previous section, idealising him or her as a benevolent "always there" object, and later idealising the forum itself (which only reflects our inner contents and projections). Just as Winnicott describes the capacity to be alone by working through the continuity between self and other, and eventually internalising the other, we internalise the other forum members as imaginary friends. The participant in the virtual group feels that "I am alone and at the same time I am not alone".

The Internet is an endless Winnicottian potential space providing a playground for people to play with ideas, interactions, closeness and distance (E-ntimacy© as will be described later), creativity, and different self-states.

A large group with the illusion of a small group: listserve and forum dynamics

Introducing the group psychotherapy discussion list

Hello, I've been lurking in the shadows for a while now. It's time to come out, encouraged by another colleague who just joined the group. I'm a mental health therapist at New Mexico State University. I'm being trained in psychodrama. I also run a psychodrama group at the Counseling Center in the University. If there are any psychodramatists out there please let me know. I'll share insights and ask questions as appropriate to this group. (Personal communication, group psychotherapy discussion list, 20 February 1996)

Hi,

I am a new member having been on the list for a few days and I have been trying to get the thread of the ongoing discussions.

My name is Moustafa Habib. I am a psychiatrist and I am at present working as the Senior Consultant Psychiatrist and am Head of Psychiatric Services in one of the Persian Gulf Sultanates. I have been doing groups for the last 18 years and find this forum most interesting. I look forward to learning from the cross-cultural and world-wide experiences. (Personal communication, Group Psychotherapy discussion list, 26 Jun 1998)

Hello dear friends.

I do not know what is my title; a lurker, a seeker, an observer, a pupil, or . . .? I am a non-academic therapist from Finland. Done private and grouptherapy for over twenty years. Using Gestalt therapy, transpersonal psychotherapy, encounter and awareness techniques. I have written several books.

I am only caretaker for my children, and one dog. I am forty years old child. I am quite swamped with all my duties (also collecting material for my next book).

This is why I am a silent pupil here in right back corner. Following your discussions sometimes; to learn.

Now I have to go back with homework. If you want to get a bit English information on me, you can look at my photo on my web page (the address in my sig).

See you later" (Personal communication, Group Psychotherapy discussion list, 25 Apr 1997)

Ok, ok . . .

After months of lurking, I feel that I should come out of the shadows for just a minute. I decided to "step to the edge" after I realized how much I missed reading other people's postings during this noticeable hiatus.

My name is Chou Chang, and I'm about to enter a master's program in community-cross cultural counseling. I just completed a 6 month group as a client, and during that period of participating in group, found this list serv [sic] one day. The more I sat in group, the more I found myself equally fascinated by the general interactions and overall process of group psychotherapy. My lurking was an attempt to understand the process more fully, and I have been learning a great deal from what people have said here. Your words have been especially helpful as I've been reflecting on my decision to pursue a career in counseling.

I'm really looking forward to lurk . . . er, I mean learning some more . . .

Warmly, (Personal communication, Group Psychotherapy discussion list, 4 Jun 1997)

The above quotes are taken from the communication some years ago on the group psychotherapy *listserve*, an Internet forum started by me in 1995 with the purpose of exchanging information with other group therapists around the world. These introductions of *listserve* (=group) members show the diversity of people joining Internet forums and set up the stage to understand their dynamics. For those who are unfamiliar with Internet terms let me explain that a *listserve* is a forum where any subscriber gets all the e-mails sent to the server by the forum members, and any e-mail s/he sends to the server is distributed to all the members as well. Nowadays there are *listserves* about almost any subject, from gardening to the movies of Woody Allen.

I described that beginning of the group psychotherapy *listserve* in the introduction of this book, including how I started understanding that it resembles my therapy groups (Weinberg, 2001). Before going any further, I want to clarify that I confine my analysis to Internet discussion lists of mental health professionals (especially the group-psychotherapy discussion list based at www.group-psychotherapy.com, which will be titled the group psychotherapy list hereby), and to un-moderated and unstructured large groups (*un-moderated* on the Internet means that no one controls the flow of information, *unstructured* means that the group does not have a clear set of rules about the communication and that the boundaries are blurred). As we will see later, large groups can be an important instrument for studying social forces and inter-group relations in society at large. As Pat de Maré (1975) put it, "the large group ... offers us a context and a possible tool for exploring the interface between the polarised and split areas of psychotherapy and sociotherapy" (p. 146). He recommends exploration of "meetings of the same members over a considerable time, and not simply a sudden short burst of meetings", as is usually done in conferences or plenary meetings. Discussion lists on the Internet provide such an opportunity. People "meet" for a prolonged period of time (as long as they are subscribed to the list), exchange ideas, communicate around their field of interest, and engage in social interaction. Although these meetings lack the rigorous group-analytic frame, and are not meant to be therapeutic (but neither are large groups, see Weinberg & Schneider, 2003), we can still learn a lot from them about the dynamics of large groups, inter-group interactions, and social conflicts. The social insight and elucidation of current unconscious social assumptions that de Maré (1975) mentions as developing in large groups, shows itself clearly in virtual reality.

Psychological processes and mechanisms in online communication

Boundaries

Boundaries in a group create safety and a sense of stability, and contribute to the developing intimacy and the ability of the participants to develop trust and open themselves. The Internet is a virtual space with no boundaries. From a psychological point of view, it can be seen as a giant, boundless potential space (Winnicott, 1987) for reality and fantasy, playing and imagination, closeness and alienation. The Internet does not have a beginning or an end. This means that the space boundaries that are well kept in a face-to-face group become vague and meaningless in Cyberspace. Other boundaries that have importance and guard a face-to-face group are the time boundaries. A session begins at a known hour and ends at a well-known time. Time boundaries are meaningless in a discussion list. One can say that in a discussion list the group has no beginning and no end regarding time, and it continues without limits.

MacKenzie (1997) points out seven boundary structures in the group: external group boundary, leadership boundary, therapist boundary, personal boundary of the individual member, interpersonal boundaries, intrapsychic boundaries, and subgroup boundaries. The external group boundaries are surely looser on the Internet than with a face-to-face group, while other boundaries need closer examination (see Chapter Five).

Issues of members joining or leaving the group and relationship(s) of members outside the group are related to questions of boundaries. Clearly these are issues in which an Internet group is markedly different from a face-to-face group. In a group that meets face-to-face, every newcomer is noticed, and the group usually reacts to this change. In fact, one of the dynamics in groups that reflects a family, occurs when a newcomer joins the group and evokes sibling envy. The new person is perceived as a younger brother or sister that is born into the family.

Leaving the group also differs in virtual vs. face-to-face groups. People can leave the Internet discussion list without anyone noticing them, which cannot occur in a group where people see one another. In a way it resembles large group meetings where you do not notice when people are missing in a session or left the group. The disappearance of the people who leave creates very different dynamics and can add to some denial of loss. Some forum leaders (e.g., on the GASi *listserve*) try to overcome this problem by letting the group know when someone signs off. In my opinion it means that these forum leaders are trying to force the virtual group to behave like a face-to-face one, instead of accepting the fact that Internet groups have different dynamics and characteristics sometimes. I related to the leader's approach in Chapter Five.

Newcomers to the list

People joining the group psychotherapy forum are requested to introduce themselves. Not everyone follows this recommendation. When it does occur, usually such an introduction to the list brings various responses. Sometimes the newcomer faces a warm welcome from veterans, sometimes her/his introduction produces questions and interesting new threads. There are other times, often when the list is absorbed in a hot discussion, when the newcomer is totally ignored.

The behaviour of the newcomer can remind us of the typical patterns of those who join a real group. Some are silent, and their presence is unnoticed. Some want to know the norms of the list first, before they post. Others send their messages immediately and can even become very involved in the discussion and take their share in a large volume of the posts. As it happens in a regular group, such a situation can stir up the old members who feel as if the newcomer is ignoring and not respecting the group's history and its veterans.

Leaving the group

Participation in the list can be terminated without the group knowing about it, just by sending a sign-off command to the server. As said above, this is where the similarity to a real group ends, as in reality no one can leave a face-to-face group without being noticed. In an effort to make the list closer to reality some sentences have been added to the group psychotherapy welcome messages ("the contract") asking people to announce their intention to leave the list and to let the others say farewell. Still only a few members do it, and usually such an announcement is accompanied by some disappointment or criticism about the function of the list (e.g., too much time spent on minor issues). The responses of the participants to that criticism are usually defensive and retaliative. When someone leaves the list after a long time of participation, and therefore her/his name is familiar, then her/his termination evokes intense responses too, as in real groups.

Here is an example to a letter of termination of a list member:

> Listmates,
>
> A while ago there was some discussion about list members making a brief statement of explanation/farewell before signing off this list. Even before that discussion I was considering signing off, but it made me more aware of all the people who leave groups and what they take with them—the voice of the non-member. So, I want to speak with that voice here by saying that I will be signing off on Friday, January 8. If the group had not touched me I would not take the time to write this. And it is not written without ambivalence. While I am probably not as enthusiastic about the way this list has functioned as some other writers have been, I have developed a fondness for its style and for many of the contributors. It would be nice to have you in my non-cyber life. (personal communication, group psychotherapy discussion list, 4 January 1999)

Outside the list communication

In group therapy there is usually a recommendation not to be involved in social relationships with members of the group. The purpose of this norm is that the therapeutic work be done in the group. Outside the group contact can be interpreted as "an attack on the group boundaries". Yalom (1995) claims that a subgroup created outside the group can achieve higher precedence over the relationships in the group. Even if there is no instruction for group members to not associate outside the group, it is usually recommended that participants bring events happening outside between group members and deal with them in the group.

Are there parallel processes in the discussion list? Certainly. List members can write to each other outside the list. It often happens that someone writing to the list receives responses to her/his private e-mail box. I estimate this as a large-scale phenomenon. It is possible to speak about "the group outside the group". Usually this does not affect the group cohesion, but sometimes there are events that have an impact on the list atmosphere.

There are various responses to private communication outside the list. Some see it as a threat to the list integrity. The threat exists only if there are concrete subgroups that might split the list and create conflicts of interests among them. Some react by feeling excluded, as if they are not important enough to take part in the outside discussion. When someone reports about an insulting private e-mail, the group tries its best to bring these letters to public discussion.

Another possibility of creating a group outside the list is by real meetings. Such meetings probably happen among members who live in the same neighbourhood and belong to the same professional community. In a group of mental health professionals there is an opportunity for face-to-face meetings at conferences, whether they are local or international.

The group psychotherapy list established a tradition of encounters among the list members participating in the annual meeting of the AGPA in the USA, and the international group psychotherapy conferences of the IAGP. These meetings have a special impact on list life, especially as they were initiated and encouraged by the list manager. Although these meetings suit the purpose of the list to encourage and nurture international collegial relationships, they still bring out several emotional reactions including anger, jealousy, and feelings of exclusion.

The first time such a meeting was initiated by the list manager (1997 in New York), some of the members not participating in the meeting wrote about the danger of a coalition between the leader and some of the members. A partial solution to this problem was to write a full report to the list about this meeting, so that everyone could share the experience. The list manager also took pictures and presented them on the Internet for every list member to see.

Contract

Usually a group works according to a contract or an agreement presented by the leader. The contract sets the rules and the boundaries (times, confidentiality, etc.) and thus structures the frame of work and creates primary safety. Without a contract it is impossible to relate to breaking the contract and the leader cannot highlight behaviours that deviate from it and interpret them.

The contract in the discussion list is unclear. In some *listserves*, every member subscribed to the list automatically gets a welcome letter specifying the contents that can be discussed and requiring fulfilling some basic rules. The rules are connected to the use of the Internet, such as not using the forum for illegal or commercial purposes. On the group psychotherapy forum, the necessity of keeping confidentiality of patients in the discussion list is mentioned too. After years of experience, it is my opinion that the contract is too open and does not clarify enough what is "right" and what is "wrong" during the participation in the forum. This might have an effect on the boundaries of the list, an issue that was discussed earlier. From time to time questions such as "is it a therapy group?" or "are personal letters allowed to be sent to the list?" arise on the list. One might think that this is the result of an unclear contract, but actually such questions can be heard in any group.

Group roles

Roles emerge in every group quite from the beginning, and some of them are crucial for the functioning of the group. Some roles facilitate the ability of the group to work on specific issues or dilemmas that are universal and emerge in any group. The most common roles in a group are those that serve the task and the emotional functions. Most writers about groups describe several other roles as well. For example, Rutan, Stone, and Shay (2007) named the structural, sociable, divergent and cautionary roles. I prefer to follow Beck's (1981) taxonomy because she attributes leader's roles to members that usually we do not see as positive leaders at all (e.g., the scapegoat leader). The four roles she identifies are: task leader, emotional leader, scapegoat leader, and defiant leader.

All these roles can be identified in an Internet forum as well. For example, the *task leader* reminds the group members to adhere to the task of the group. In a *listserve*, where the contract is vague (see above) and the discussion can go astray, it is important that someone will gently bring the group back to the track, and it is always better that a member of the group does it rather than the list moderator, who contains enough projections about his/her authority anyway.

Here is an e-mail from such a task leader (a member of the group) posted after the terrible shooting event in Newtown, Connecticut (December, 2012), was discussed on the group psychotherapy list:

> I think B.'s post that the mass shootings at Newtown act as a Rorschach-like stimulus influencing our individual postings makes a lot of sense.
>
> <snip>
>
> The List group-oriented discussion has been premised on social unconscious conceptualizations and, as G. pointed out, these can become reductionist despite intentions to the contrary. Now we seem to have a diversion to G-d/Satan. To what purpose? What are the dynamics of our discussion from a group standpoint? I don't have a clue.
>
> <snip>
>
> For those of you doing groups, has Newtown entered your groups—and in what form, plus how have you intervened, particularly given the reality/possibility of strong CT on our parts?
>
> Thanks for reading—very interested in your responses, particularly re ongoing groups. (Personal communication, group psychotherapy discussion list, 20 December 2012)

Another role that can be identified in the Internet forum is the *defiant leader*. According to Beck (1981) this member monitors the boundary between participating as a "group member" and an "autonomous individual", between the pull to cohesiveness and pushing back from intense involvement. He or she warns the group against the power of the leader, and reminds us that leaders are always in danger of abusing their power. In an Internet group, where the moderator has the power to censor messages, and where self and others boundaries can merge, it is crucial that such a leader should emerge from among the members.

Here is a message from a group psychotherapy forum member who continuously chose a challenging defiant leader position towards both the moderator of the group (myself) and the other group members. In fact, because of the sarcastic way she wrote her messages sometimes, it was a challenge for me as the list moderator to keep in mind that she was doing a service for the group by her comments.

Haim,

It is interesting that in your reactive reply to S. you move from an I to a We. Is it difficult for you to remain in the I-position and enter into a dialogue with S's I? A lecture does little to impact others and is a "yellow card" of sorts.

I find it interesting that you did not react to Ms. H's use of abusive language on several occasions. Help me understand your refrain.

I also ask that you help me understand your use of the word "best" [the writer is cynically referring to my signing e-mails with the word "best" as an abbreviation for "best regards". H.] when ending a seemingly personal note. What are you trying to say when using the word "best?"

I look forward to a scholarly reply. (Personal communication, group psychotherapy discussion list, 23 June 2010)

One of the dangerous situations in a group (and a good example of regressive primitive aggression) is when the whole group finds a *scapegoat* to attack. In this situation the group projects its "badness" on the scapegoated individual, hoping to get rid of split-off unwanted inner parts by attacking or expelling the scapegoat from the group. Yalom (1995) sees this situation as endangering the integrity of the group and requiring the leader's intervention. Corey (1995) suggests that the leader turn the attention of the attacking members to their inner worlds and what is going on inside them.

Such a situation also occurs in a discussion list. It can happen when someone "draws the fire" of the members by a certain irritating or provocative style of writing, by posting too frequently, or by an extremely annoying response. The scapegoat also can be chosen for this role because of a certain weakness (e.g., inexperience with groups, in the case of group psychotherapy). In these instances there are many impulsive attacks on the individual, as if the whole discussion list has turned against that person. While conflicts and disagreements arise in almost every group, usually when someone is attacked, some people will defend the attacked person. One of the signs that a scapegoat process is developing is that no one defends the one who is attacked. Perhaps since the emotional reactions of the attacked person on the list are unseen, the aggression increases. It is important that the forum moderator keeps in mind Beck's (1981) ideas about the *scapegoat leader*, mentioned before, and remember that a scapegoat leader helps the forum to define certain identity boundaries of the group as a system and its ability to contain and accept a wide range of differences. In the virtual space of a boundless group, defining these boundaries is even more important than in a face-to-face one.

Projection and other psychological mechanisms

Projection

Suler (1999) describes how people connected to Cyberspace "often feel—consciously or subconsciously—that they are entering a "place" or "space" that is filled with a wide array of meanings and purposes" (p. 1). It almost goes without saying that the central psychological mechanism working in Internet communication is projection. With the lack of visual and auditory cues, and with only textual signs to create an impression, the readers complete a lot of missing data with their imagination, thus projecting their inner world upon the written text. Suler (1996) writes: "Because the experience of the other person often is limited to text, there is a tendency for the user to project a variety of wishes, fantasies, and fears onto the ambiguous figure at the other end of cyberspace" (p. 1).

It is interesting to note that, examining the ideal conditions for the traditional psychoanalytic setting, we find that the conditions on the Internet suit it well. Perhaps the idea of psychoanalysis online is not so blasphemous. The online psychoanalyst is totally unseen and unheard and only her/his words appear on the screen. These are ideal conditions for the psychoanalyst to become a blank screen and a target for projections.

Here is an example of the effect of the signatures of the people writing on the list, manifesting the reader's projections:

> As many of those who have been around as long as I have or longer know, I come awake when the threads contain personal reflection, stories, case situations, and practical topics. I shy away from (intim-idated) from the more academic, jargons, intellectual subjects. Although the M.D.s and Ph.D.s on the forum for the most part "real" people [sic], my lack of degrees (and knowledge of the "pub-lished works", reference materials, etc.) causes me to shy away for

fear of asking the "dumb" question. So, I read these threads, learn much, but often feel alone in the group. (Personal communication, group psychotherapy discussion list, 14 November 1998).

The absence of cues other than the written text offers many sources for projections. In face-to-face interaction people rely on the combination of textual, visual, auditory, and even olfactory cues to interpret the meaning of the speaker's sentences. This is so common that people do not notice how important each of these dimensions is to (what they think is) an exact understanding of the speaker. In addition, the listener usually uses body gestures (such as head nodding) and facial expressions to convey her listening and check whether she is still attuned to the speaker, creating a feedback loop.

If we take out the visual component from daily communication (e.g., in a phone conversation) we still have the voice and its nuances to tell us if the intention was humorous, sad, or sarcastic. All these subliminal and subtle cues disappear in Cyberspace communication. The Internet leaves the written word as the only source of interpretation and this leads to many misunderstandings. People very easily interpret neutral sentences as hostile or hurting, and might respond back in aggression to this misinterpretation. A lot of word-wars (called "flaming" on the Internet) start in discussion lists and forums when a comment that was meant to be humorous is conceived as insulting by the reader.

The following is an exchange of letters on the group psychotherapy list exemplifying well this phenomenon:

I have noticed that you use "Hmmmm" a lot and it is confusing to me what it might signify in each instance. I don't know if it is your intention, but to me it comes across as smugness disguising anger, and perhaps detracts from more important aspects of some of your posts. (Personal communication, group psychotherapy discussion list, 12 December 1999)

(I assume that most of you reading the above sentences have the association of the "hmmm" that Rogerian psychotherapists use in order to show their empathy. It is interesting to note that this "Hmmm" on the Internet is not interpreted as empathic at all).

To which the member responds:

In fact, whenever, I type the "hmmmmmmm . . ." it is to indicate that I am giving further thought to what has been said and need time to put these thoughts into the proper form for this group. I am actually slightly surprised that you felt my above reply seemed angry because I am not really angry. (Personal communication, group psychotherapy discussion list, 12 December 1999)

Yet another responds:

For what it's worth, my own mental image when you've used "hmmmm", is that of my mother with arms crossed, foot tapping, and staring at me with an accusing glare . . .: "So the cookie's were here this morning, they're all gone now, but you didn't eat them? Hmmm . . ." (Personal communication, group psychotherapy discussion list, 13 December 1999)

Not only projections govern the scene in Internet forums. *Projective identification* mechanisms also appear in these discussions, although they are more difficult to notice. In times of heated discussion, they are easier to identify. When "flaming" starts, they sweep away many members of the forum, driving mature adults into regressive behaviour, impulsive reactions and disrespecting sentences. The hostility felt in the list is projected onto the members and they identify with it and become hostile themselves. This process makes it difficult to identify who is the attacker and who is the attacked. The confusion is so strong that in the same letter one can find reflective, wise advice intertwined with insulting remarks. The following two sentences appeared on the same e-mail.

May I, as politely as I can, suggest that when you have a strong emotional response that you take time and give a little more thought before you respond,

together with,

I thought you either have to be very young and inexperienced or very rude and insulting. (Personal communication, group psychotherapy discussion list, 7 March 2001)

Regression

Regressive processes are evident in therapy groups, expressed in the use of archaic defences, regression to early object relations, and dependency on the leader and the group. For example, the unclear situation of the forming stage creates regression (Rutan, Stone, & Shay, 2007), and the members expect the leader to rescue them from the anxiety of not knowing what is expected. Regression is also often seen in discussion lists. Holland (1996) observed three symptoms of regression on the Internet. The first symptom is primitive aggression that finds its expression in defamation wars and heated debate. Another symptom is sexual harassment such as crude invitations to people about whom one knows no more than their online signatures. The last one is extraordinary generosity: total strangers will give up hours of their time to send one another research data. People who have never met face-to-face are ready to help one another in many practical ways just because of their Internet acquaintance. The reader might wonder why generosity is considered regression. The reason is that people do not activate the same reality testing they use in face-to-face communication, and expose their vulnerability in a way that blurs boundaries between self and others (Weinberg, 2006). The anonymity of the writer and the immediacy of response in e-mail encourage regression.

Transference

All the authors writing about group therapy dedicate many paragraphs to transference in the group (Fehr, 1999; Rutan, Stone, & Shay, 1993; Yalom, 1995). Transference in the group exists towards the leader, the members in the group, and the group as a whole. What makes the group unique is the possibility of multiple simultaneous transferences. Because the Internet has no audio-visual cues, it encourages massive projections onto the writer and onto the meaning of what is written. Suler (1996) writes: "Because the experience of the other person often is limited to text, there is a tendency for the user to project a variety of wishes, fantasies, and fears onto the ambiguous figure at the other end of cyberspace".

Every reader on the list creates an inner image of the writing participants. The image can be of the writer's age, appearance, character, or even gender. Foreign names also provide a challenge to the readers. The reader develops a personal attitude towards each of the regular writers on the list. For example, a person may immediately delete some writers' posts without even reading them, because they are usually irritating or boring. Other writers might have qualities such as wisdom, experience, or impulsiveness attributed to them. The transference to the list manager was addressed in Chapter Five.

Mirroring

Mirroring is an important component in both individual therapy, greatly emphasised in self-psychology (Kohut, 1971) and, in group therapy, greatly emphasised in group analysis (Foulkes, 1964). On the surface, e-mail communication lacks any mirroring. In a previous chapter we discussed the consequences of this missing mirroring and how it is related to neurobiology and mirror neurons. Lack of mirroring leads to no validation or acknowledgement of the writer's expression. This is a typical large group phenomenon (see Weinberg & Schneider, 2003), which leads to the next topic:

Large group or small group dynamics

The question to be discussed here is whether phenomena familiar from therapy groups also occur on the Internet discussion list. More specifically, does a discussion list essentially resemble a large group, or are the phenomena more similar to those encountered in a small group? Those two kinds of group sometimes show different dynamics (see Weinberg & Schneider, 2003). We should also consider another possibility, which is that Internet groups are more like a fishbowl where a small number of members of a larger group participate, while the larger membership watches quietly.

Is it a large group?

Let us first look at the definitions of the large group to see if the Internet group fits this definition. One way of distinguishing between a small, median, and large group is simply by its numbers. A small group can be up to fifteen people. Fifteen to twenty-five participants compose a median group (de Maré, Piper, & Thompson, 1991) and from twenty-five or thirty-five on we are dealing with a large group. If we follow this criterion, surely an Internet group is usually a large group as it is composed of many, sometimes even hundreds of people.

But clearly, defining a psychological construct such as a large group only by the number of people present in the room (or registered on the *listserve*) is not recommended, as it is based on superficial surface elements. In addition, the fact is that not all of the members subscribed participate in every discussion. My definition of the large group follows Turquet's observation that notes: ". . . with such numbers the group can no longer be face to face" (1975, p. 88). Accordingly, my practical-structural definition of the large group can be, "Any group with such a large number of participants they cannot be encompassed in a single glance" (Weinberg, 2003b). This makes Internet groups large groups by definition, because people cannot see one another at all, and so the actual number of registered members is not important to the participants. This definition stresses the importance of seeing everyone in a group. Seeing everyone is essential to have the intimacy typical in small group dynamics.

Much has been written about the dynamics of large groups. Schiff and Glassman (1969) describe some variables found as group size increases. They include an increased tendency to subgrouping, less opportunity for the individual to speak, dilution of affectionate ties, decreased familiarity with others, skewed participation with more active leaders and very silent members, and a greater threat to the individual. De Maré, Piper, and Thompson (1991) argue that large groups are experienced as intimidating, inhibiting, and frustrating. At first it might be difficult for the individual to find a voice and a place. They also indicate that topics that come up in the large group include social and macro-cultural aspects that are part of the human condition, such as illness, death, class, race, politics, etc. In his paper "The Internet and the large group", Davidson (1998) concludes that the communication processes within a discussion list can be likened to the dynamics of the large group, a developing interface between intrapsychic, interpersonal, political, professional, cultural, and societal reflective exploration.

The main phenomenon on Internet forums reminding us of large group dynamics is actually related to the lack of mirroring mentioned in the previous paragraph. Oftentimes, participants in the large group hear no echo and receive no response to what they say (sometimes after long hesitation about expressing their voice). When a person's message brings no response whatsoever, the person feels as if her/his voice disappears in Cyberspace, which adds to the feeling of being lost in the crowd (Weinberg & Schneider, 2003). This is similar to the threat to the individual identity in the large group described by Turquet (1975). When the list disregards them, people can feel hurt, or insignificant, and sometimes they retaliate in anger. "Am I so unimportant and are my words so meaningless" the writer asks himself/herself? (Weinberg, 2003b).

> I too am impacted when my words seem to vanish into cyberspace, feeling unheard, insignificant, small, etc. I have discovered that when this happens I either shrink away quietly for a while or come back "yelling louder". (Personal communication, group psychotherapy discussion list, 14 November 1998).

It seems that alienation and the feeling of being only "a cog in the machine" arise when the individual is ignored. It is difficult for the individual to find her/his unique place in this virtual group, just as it happens in a large group, and people feel the threat of a loss of self.

> I wonder why I feel this anxiety here—in fact, in relation to this group, I wonder about that a lot. I think it's related to N.'s observation about having some difficulty finding a place in the group. I, too, have had this experience, along with the sense that there is some banter between the "core" members that I don't understand (thank you N., for putting words to this). It's a feeling of having my nose pressed up against a glass, wanting to be inside but not quite knowing where the door is (and would I have the sense to walk over to it and turn the knob if I did know where it was?) I know myself and groups well enough to know that this is about me much more than it is about the members of the group; nonetheless the fact that this is happening in an electronic group fascinates me. (Personal communication, group psychotherapy discussion list, 8 January 1999)

> I also have felt the impact of the V O I D when there is no response to a particular post of mine. Sometimes I imagine that there is at least one of the lurker members (300+) that is responding in positively though in silence. I am not sure why I often connect lack of response to negative feelings . . ... (Personal communication, group psychotherapy discussion list, 29 March 2001)

These vignettes clarify that the difficulty in finding a voice, the intimidation by the crowd, the anxiety facing the mass, and the confusion produced by so many voices exists on the list in the same way as seen in the large group.

A superficial overview of the discussion list e-mail exchange strengthens the impression of a large group as it shows resemblance to what we see in face-to-face ones. The multiplicity of voices and themes expressed in a forum creates a sense of confusion and over-whelming flood. Connecting to Cyberspace is often related to a sense of alienation. Conflictual situations and emotional intensity with regressive tendencies may take control of the situation. At first it seems risky to send a message to the net and find one's voice and identity in that crowd.

Yet another issue that resembles the face-to-face large group arises from the vast number of subjects discussed in parallel and in a seem-ingly unrelated manner. There is a feeling that people do not listen to one another. It is difficult to follow one "thread" (a common Internet expression for a chain of letters on one theme), as there can be many voices—a written cacophony—at the same time. Some of the members might react with overwhelmed silence.

People seem surprisingly vulnerable to feeling ignored and misun-derstood, and even narcissistically injured. In response to this trau-matic experience, the group seems to aggregate and then to seek homogeneity until the list regains its experience of cohesion and coherence, and a work group is re-established, a sequence identical to the process that Hopper (1997) described in large analytical groups.

Another salient and dangerous feature of large groups is their tendency to use primitive defence mechanisms such as splitting and projective identification, resulting in a paranoid atmosphere, aggres-sive expressions, and the deterioration of communication into mean-inglessness. "Since the large group is by its very size frustrating—it generates hate" (De Maré, Piper, & Thompson, 1991, p. 18). In some lists this is what happens. In a forum open to the public, discussing psychological issues (psychology forum on IOL—Israel-On-Line) one of the participants started sending volumes of insulting and aggres-sive messages to the members. The members who were hurt retaliated with counter attacks or with affront. The atmosphere became heated, nobody listened to the other, and it seemed as if a dialogue was impossible. The result was that the forum manager had to close it for some days and reopened it with new and strict rules about approved messages.

Most of the time the group psychotherapy discussion list has developed different norms for communicating, which show mutual respect. This may have happened because the members on this list are mature mental health professionals who are aware of process and are comfortable with discussing it whenever a problem arises. There are deeper dynamics on the group psychotherapy list involved with this avoidance of primitive aggression so typical of the Internet and large group, relating to the norms (some of which the participants are unaware) of a community of mental health helpers. However, at times, even this relatively professional forum exploded with "flame-wars". Interestingly enough, (in my experience), it happened around social issues and inter-national conflicts.

What is unique in the group psychotherapy list is that the members can observe the process and relate to it, as they are experienced group therapists themselves. Here is an example of a post to the list about the process:

> The thread that D., C. and I have followed about participation in the "List Group" has led to some reflections on my experiences with this List. I had some expectations about being in conversations with other professionals about leading groups and group dynamics. I have found it hard to identify the norms of this List. Some members seem to know each other well from association on the List, and also from meeting at conferences. This outside contact changes the dynamic in a "group" among those members. The topics change so rapidly that it is difficult for me to internally process what has been said before it has changed.
>
> I also have observed the differences in perspectives about the role of the "group leader" and the differences in therapeutic schools of thought. These often seem unacknowledged in the comments that are made, and I wonder if we talk past each other at times when the differences are not acknowledged. This List seems to be most helpful to me when it discusses a specific topic. (Personal communication, group psychotherapy discussion list, 8 November 1998)

Or is it a small group?

So far we examined how the Internet group resembles a large group, but at other times, what is seen on a discussion list on the Internet is different from what is expected in a large group. The large group makes it difficult to create significant interpersonal relationships between members and develop intimacy among them. Earl Hopper

(1997) described the fourth basic assumption of aggregation/massification. When this basic assumption is active, and it is usually intensively active in a large group, there is no room for the individual and no place for the voice of uniqueness. Extrapolating then one should expect only a small amount of self-disclosure on the list, and only a few responses to any that occurs. Self-disclosure on the Internet is not anticipated also because the level of safety in the boundless virtual world is supposed to be low since the boundaries of time and space in a discussion group, so typical of a face-to-face analytic group, do not exist. Each member sends posts whenever seems appropriate to him or her, and reads the messages on the list in his or her own time. Members enter the list or leave it all the time and the writer has no idea about who is a member in the list at a specific time, and who else might read the posts in addition to the regular members. So clearly, there are many barriers to feeling the necessary safety for self-disclosure.

Based on the above assumptions, the high level of personal revelation on the list is quite unexpected. For example, the group psychotherapy discussion list is perceived as a cohesive community with which many of its members feel deeply involved. The list is meaningful to their professional life and beyond. Members create relationships that they experience as close and intimate. People share painful events with one another, for example, death and dying of self and others, chronic and acute illness, career crises, and more, receiving many empathic and caring responses.

An example of the emotional tone seen on the list is an event when one of the members lost his newborn son. He wrote a very touching letter to the list about it. Here is a short paragraph from it.

> My heart is broken—words can't convey the grief, and I realize only now that the depth of this pain is beyond comprehension. I feel waves of horrible sadness and utter bewilderment. I'm sure that anger will come, though it has not yet shown itself. (Personal communication, group psychotherapy discussion list, 2 July 2000)

A flood of responses followed his e-mail all emotionally sharing their condolences and personal losses.

> Tears are falling as I write this, this "wet strength" reflecting the passion of your connection to and loss of your newborn son. (Personal communication, group psychotherapy discussion list, 2 July 2000).

> I have not been responding to the many threads that have been
> happening here—but, your post arrested me. I grieve with you. I
> cannot imagine a deeper pain than that associated with the loss of
> a child. (Personal communication, group psychotherapy discus-
> sion list, 3 July 2000).

It is an important issue to attempt an understanding of how
members of this large group manage to ignore its vastness and still
feel safe enough to write such personal letters.

Although many of the participants have never met each other face
to face, they can develop emotions towards each other, feel close or
angry and even despise some of the members just from reading their
posts. Here is an example of an e-mail sent to the list about the feeling of belonging to this group:

> Just a few days ago I came to a STARTLING REALIZATION. I read all
> of the messages faithfully and I have come to the conclusion that
> I have been considering the list like a real, live group. That is,
> even though I wasn't speaking up, that you all "knew" I was in
> the room. Since I could "see" and "hear" all of you (through your
> posts), I assumed that you were all aware of my presence. That is
> why I decided to write. I want you to be aware of my presence,
> even though I am often silent.

There are many other group dynamics identified in this virtual
group that look similar to those we are acquainted with in our face-
to-face small therapeutic groups. Here are some examples:

1. Parallel process: when the group discusses an issue in group
    work, the participants might enact the phenomenon they are talk-
    ing about. For example, the list is discussing what to do when
    members in therapeutic groups monopolise the sessions and at
    the same time it seems that there are monopolisers that control
    the discussion on the list.
2. Lurkers: this is an Internet expression relating to members that
    only read the e-mail and do not actively participate. This is simi-
    lar to the silent observers in a group, and when this issue is dis-
    cussed it raises the same reactions we can see in a group, from
    anger to indifference. However, one clear difference between
    Internet lurkers and silent group members is that the Internet
    group can ignore them until their presence is mentioned. It is much

harder to ignore a passive non-talking member in a small group for a long time, and in this aspect, the Internet forum resembles more of a large group, where silent people can go unnoticed.

3.   After-group connections and subgrouping: as mentioned above, in real groups there is a possibility of writing to another group member "backchannel" (privately). Even more outside of face-to-face group therapy norms, members have visited one another in their homes around the world outside of conferences. Sometimes this is revealed in the group and, as in real life, people can feel excluded (actually, the group psychotherapy group have developed a group norm to reveal these meetings).

4.   Transference: the fact that there is no non-verbal communication on the net (except for special smiling/sad signs—emoticons—to hint at the speaker's meaning), makes it a perfect place for projections and transference. The members develop an impression and emotions around the other participants.

Or perhaps it is a fishbowl group?

But perhaps a *listserve* is more like a fishbowl? The number of people participating in a discussion on a specific issue on a discussion list is usually ten to fifteen. Others, who may be observing the discussion, do not write. This is similar to a fishbowl where a subset of members participates in the discussion and the others do not intervene and only watch. Their existence might almost be forgotten. However, when we look closer into this matter, we find that in a fishbowl the boundaries are much more rigid then in the virtual space of the list, where all participants can join in whenever they want to. In fact, each issue brings new discussants to the fore. *Most of the time the list maintains an illusion of a small group and ignores the many observers*. This means that a small group gathers around every issue discussed, behaving like a small analytic group ignoring the hundreds of silent observers around them. Without writing, there is no evidence of the silent members' existence. They are easily forgotten (or rather ignored). It can also be interpreted as if the basic assumption of pairing prevails (Bion, 1959), moving a small subgroup of members to do the work for the whole list. This subgroup might have a conscious or unconscious aim of sending their posts to "save" the list from deteriorating into silence and degenerating.

As the Internet group develops, it establishes a consistent subgroup of members that participate in most of the discussions. These members seem more involved in the subjects discussed, send their messages more often, seem to create closer relationship with other members, and are perceived as more important in the life of the forum. Other people come and go, express their opinions now and then, contribute to the discussions from time to time, but this *core group* (my own term for this subgroup) continuously contributes to the ongoing vividness of the large group. As said above, I estimate this core group to consist of ten to fifteen people, and in a way they are responsible for the illusion of the small group. In order for such a subgroup to develop, the Internet forum needs time to develop a sufficient mass of people from whom this core group stands out.

Here is a message of one of the group psychotherapy forum members, summarising well the relationship between the online large group and small group.

> There are so many people here that I admire, like, love, at times hate. My style of being here varies. Sometimes I hold back, not wanting to take up too much space. There are so many threads I would like to insert myself into, but if I did my name would appear a dozen times a day. Many times I am on the periphery, or many times I am away for several days, don't read anything, and respond spontaneously to the first post that interests me when I reconnect. Then I neurose about who I might inadvertently be ignoring. I sometimes worry that it could seem like I am ignoring other posts, which I guess in some sense I am b/c I often don't get to them. Other times I don't relate to the posts, and so don't respond. Sheesh, how neurotic!

> I think this is the challenge of the large group, which I still try to make a small group by connecting to a few people at a time, even though I am aware that there could be 400 people on the list. (Personal communication, group psychotherapy discussion list, 12 January 2013).

Rippa, Moss, and Chirurg (2011) asked the same question mentioned here: "Can virtual, Internet groups, which lack visual and auditory cues, be compared to face-to-face groups, in which body language and non-verbal communication is part of the overall communication among participants?" (pp. 440–441). They counted the number of contributions to the group psychotherapy *listserve* for each member participating in a period of four months. They found that only nineteen per cent of the members post actively. They concluded: "There are many similarities between these cyberspace groups and face-to-face groups, despite the lack of visual and auditory cues in the former" (p. 441). Therefore, a discussion list is like a large group in many ways. Yet, because of the special influences of virtual reality, this large group often behaves as if it was a small group. It is *a large group in the dark, with an illusion of a small group.*

CHAPTER SEVEN

The Internet and the social unconscious: from intimacy to E-ntimacy©

More about the social unconscious

Freud described the unconscious as existing beyond space and time. The individual unconscious is not bounded by reality limitations of time and space. Bion (1959) expanded this argument to the group unconscious and its basic assumptions, claiming that time and space are ignored in the group unconscious. Cyberspace seems as if it was originated in order to explore the unconscious because it is the ultimate boundless-timeless environment where conventional reality's rules do not exist. It can become a place to explore utopian possibilities, or a wrecking yard for traditional culture. Knowing how the internet is perceived as a boundless space, and how online forums exist beyond time limitations, it is only natural to wonder whether the Internet becomes a fertile ground for the creation of a new kind of unconscious: the Internet unconscious.

But before entering the realm of the Internet unconscious, already knowing how boundaries differ in different cultures and that online forums resemble large group in some ways (see previous chapters), perhaps we should explore what is written about the large group unconscious, and especially what we know already about the unconscious of people in social large groups.

The social unconscious (Hopper, 2003; Hopper & Weinberg, 2011; Weinberg, 2007 refers to the existence and constraints of social, cultural, and communication arrangements of which people are to varying degrees "unaware". It includes shared anxieties, fantasies, defences, and object relations, as well as various aspects of socio-cultural-economic-political factors and forces, many of which are also co-constructed unconsciously by the members of particular groupings.

Many people understand this concept as if it means that society has an unconscious. However, this interpretation is problematic since society is not an organism, does not have a brain, and if we attribute some unconscious properties to the social system, it is unclear where it resides. Therefore, there are two non-exclusive ways to understand this concept. The first interpretation is to see the social unconscious as part of the individual unconscious. Looking from this perspective, we view and analyse the unconscious impact of those social arrangements mentioned above on the individual, thus focusing on the unconscious way in which people in a specific society are influenced in a similar way by it. The social unconscious can be understood as the internalisation of social facts, norms, and cultural aspects that we are unaware of, including the representation of social forces and power relations in our psyche (Dalal, 2001). In fact, when we look at the social unconscious this way, it is unclear whether we should separate the social unconscious from the individual unconscious. Indeed Knauss (2006, p. 163) claims that "There is no such thing as 'the group unconscious', the 'social unconscious or a collective, cultural unconscious'. Instead, each individual's unconscious is groupal." From this point of view, we emphasise how the social unconscious is embedded in and becomes an inseparable part of the individual unconscious.

Another way to understand the social unconscious is through the relational/inter-subjective perspective (Mitchell, 1993). "Relational theory is based on the shift from the classical idea that it is the patient's mind that is being studied (where mind is thought as independently and autonomously within the boundaries of the individual) to the relational notion that mind is inherently dyadic, social, interactional, and interpersonal" (Aron, 1996, p. x). The relational/inter-subjective conceptualisation suggests a different reading of the unconscious and the way we understand it in addition to the regular Freudian one. We are not talking about specific contents located in a certain area that exists a priori and that we help by illuminating in therapy. We are talking about creating the unconscious and acquiring "knowledge" about it with the help of the other through conversation. This co-created unconscious is an infinite, conversational, open system (Mitchell, 1993), or as Tubert-Oklander (2006) termed it, "free-floating conversation". This point of view relates to the inter-subjective field in which the social unconscious seems to reside, and to its co-creation by people of the same society. Here we emphasise how the social unconscious is a transpersonal phenomenon, part of the foundation matrix (Foulkes, 1990) of a specific culture. It reminds us of the relational unconscious (see Altman, 2010; Gerson, 2004; Safran, 2006) that is lately discussed more and more in the inter-subjective psychoanalytic literature (for a more detailed discussion about these two aspects see the Introduction to Hopper & Weinberg's book, 2011).

Looking at the social unconscious from this frame of reference, we can say that it resides in the potential space between people. The inter-subjective field is a co-creation of the psyche of the people involved in the interaction, meaning that it is not the simple result of the people's unconscious but is a new co-unconscious (Moreno, 1934/1978) belonging to neither of the participants. Extrapolating from two people to a group or even society, this is the space of the social unconscious.

So the social unconscious can be viewed along two orthogonal axes: The vertical axis, includes the impact of the history of a social group on the daily behaviour of people belonging to that society, especially its traumatic unelaborated historical events. The other axis is the horizontal one, which is about the inter-subjective, transpersonal aspect mentioned above. It is related to what happens among people of the same society and how they co-create and maintain the social unconscious through their daily interactions.

Inter(net)relatedness

There is more than one way to understand the connection between the social unconscious and the Internet, as these entities are interrelated. One possibility is to examine the way in which the social unconscious is reflected on the Internet. In addition, we can look at the "Internet unconscious" (see Weinberg 2003b) and describe the unique elements that compose this intercultural, international web of relationship. Yet another way of connecting between the internet and the social unconscious is exploring how the existence of the World Wide Web, and its common and ubiquitous use since its beginning, influenced our society both consciously and unconsciously.

How the Internet impacts the social unconscious

As an example of this last possibility, let us explore the influence of the Internet on our ability to empathise with people from cultures we are unfamiliar with, and people who are usually perceived as strangers and "others". In his popular book *The Empathic Civilization* (2009) Jeremy Rifkin connects the development of empathy with the industrial and communication revolutions. He associates the innovation of printing, resulting in the spreading of books all over the world, with a change occurring in the human consciousness. He believes that these literary narratives made us more empathetic as the romantic literature increased human awareness to feelings, and in turn influenced the political and social changes such as the French and American revolutions. If Rifkin is right, probably the change itself was unintended and unconscious, creating a situation where a technological change led to an unconscious change in our ways of relating to one another, thus influencing the social unconscious.

Rifkin describes an expansion of the ability to become empathic with further and further distant "others" the more our means of communication developed; from a restricted empathy to blood ties in the ancient world, to identities and loyalties based on complex communication revolutions that annihilate time and space in the industrial revolution of the nineteen century. If the spread of books and reading stories about human feelings and experiences extended our ability to empathise with others, communicating with many different people, cultures, and societies over the Internet might enhance this ability as well. Participating in Internet forums can become a way to enhance empathy. Communicating with people from other countries and other cultures is the best way to break down stereotypes and overcome our unchecked assumptions about them.

According to Brown (2001), one manifestation of the social unconscious are the assumptions that unconsciously guide people's behaviours. Assumptions about human nature change in different eras: Medieval Christians' world view saw human nature as fallen and looked to salvation through God's grace. Enlightenment thinkers emphasised the idea that human beings' essential nature is rational, detached, and autonomous. They argued that individual salvation lies in unlimited material progress on Earth. These tacit assumptions were part of the social unconscious of those times.

Is the contemporary view of mankind narcissistic and non-empathic? There are contrary views of our narcissistic society. Twenge and Campbell (2009), in their book, *The Narcissism Epidemic: Living in the Age of Entitlement*, distinguish between self-esteem and narcissism, and focus on cultural narcissism that goes deep into social values. The authors argue that a narcissistic epidemic is spreading in the Western world, that we need to recognise it and its negative consequences and take corrective action.

Other authors see the young generation as far more concerned with the planetary environment and climate change and more likely to favour sustainable economic growth. Today's emerging adults see themselves as international citizens to an extent rarely experienced before. They could also be called the empathic generation. Their international experiences and education have made them more aware than any previous generation of how interconnected the world is. They are more supportive of globalisation and immigration than older generations. This younger generation is also more tolerant than any generation in history in support of gender equality and the willingness to fight for the rights of the disabled, gays and sexual minorities, and other minorities. According to the General Social Survey conducted annually by the University of Chicago, students are nearly unanimous in believing that women should have equal opportunities with men. In short, they favour a world of inclusivity over exclusivity.

This inclusivity might be derived from the impact of the Internet on the social unconscious: young people nowadays think of human nature as empathic, mindful, engaged, and driven by the interconnectedness of life. The *Homo sapien* is being eclipsed by *Homo empathicus*.

I do not ignore the fact that when one reads the comments of people on any Internet article ("talkback") it is often filled with hatred of the other, stereotypes, and no sense of empathy or perspective. Perhaps the evidence of people becoming more empathic is from elites (students). We need to remember the underbelly of the Internet as well (white supremacy groups, terrorist networks, child porn, and more).

So what is the Internet unconscious?

Looking from another perspective, we can describe "the Internet unconscious" and analyse its unique features. However, if the concept of the social unconscious is prone to misconceptions as we saw at the beginning of this chapter, the idea of the Internet unconscious is much more confusing and generates both misunderstandings and resistance. As some of the arguments against the use of the term "the social unconscious" come from the fact that society is not a living organism and as such has no brain, relating an unconscious to the Internet, with its disembodied features, at a first glance seems more than puzzling. More than that, the Internet is not a country, neither a state nor a nation, and it is questionable whether we can relate to it as a society.

Relating to the Internet unconscious does not mean that the Internet itself is an entity that has an unconscious, but that the people who use it, belong to its communities, think about it, and imagine what it looks like, have shared thoughts and fantasies about it, of which they are unaware.

The second argument, that the Internet is neither a country nor a society, ignores the fact that the Internet did develop a culture of its own. If a culture is typified by its language, then the culture of the Internet contributed many new words to the spoken language: hoaxes, chain letters, flaming, spam, Google, hackers, netiquette, lurker are all new terms or terms with specific meaning in the newly developing folklore of the net. In *Cultures of Internet*, Shields (1996) describes the main features of this culture: The Internet is supposed to be *the* ultimate democratic, egalitarian, freedom of speech culture. No one controls it, and its structure is not based on class. This is one shared fantasy people have about the Internet, and as such it is part of the Internet unconscious.

If we look for an "Internet unconscious", one possibility is that the social unconscious on the Internet reflects the unconscious of a specific forum of people who share a common field of interest. But this definition will restrict our discussion to a specific forum and a limited number of people, while we are looking for a phenomenon that reflects the foundation matrix—the deep hidden ties and assumptions connecting people wherever they are. If we elaborate on the definition of the social unconscious at the beginning of this chapter, we can say that the Internet unconscious is *the co-constructed shared unconscious of members belonging to Internet communities and cultures. It includes shared anxieties, fantasies, defences, myths, and memories about the Internet.* Brown (2001) suggested a systematic way for analysing the social unconscious of a specific society. In order to analyse the Internet unconscious and describe the ways it expresses itself, we will use his four ways of the social unconscious manifestation.

Assumptions

a. The Internet is a free democratic society—Shield's (1996) description of the Internet culture mentioned above is actually a set of assumptions about the Internet. These assumptions are taken for granted and shared by most people who think they know this media. For many, the Internet offers the hope of a more democratic society. By promoting a decentralised form of social mobilisation, it is said, the Internet can help us to renovate our institutions and liberate ourselves from our authoritarian legacies. The Internet does indeed hold these possibilities: The quick spread of demonstrations around the world in 2011–2013, in Egypt, Israel, Turkey, Brazil, and other countries, largely supported by social networks and bringing hundreds of thousands of young people to mostly quiet demonstrations, sometimes changing the regime, is a sound proof of this potential.
On the other hand, some countries, such as Iran and the People's Republic of China, restrict what people in their countries can see on the Internet, especially unwanted political and religious content. Authoritarian societies will attempt to suppress the cultural practices of networking, and democratic societies will promote them. The Internet can become a tool for social progress, but it can also become a tool of oppression or another centralised broadcast medium.
The Internet unconscious contains an illusionary belief that ultimate freedom of speech is achieved in Cyberspace and that forum members always show respect and tolerance to different opinions.
b. Internet forums are similar to face-to-face small groups—in the virtual environment on Internet discussion lists and forums, the communication might look like the kind of interaction we are used to in small groups, but the participant's fantasy creates an intra-psychic process. As we discussed earlier, virtual groups on Cyberspace are large groups with an illusion of small groups.

c.   People and machines are essentially different—Turkle (1995) claims that as human beings become increasingly intertwined with the technology and with each other via the technology, old distinctions about what is specifically human and specifically technological become more complex. The more people spend time in Cyberspace and create technologically enmeshed relationships, we might ask to what extent they have become cyborgs, transgressive mixtures of biology and technology. Haraway (1985) explored the interfaces between human/machine/animal/information and deduced from them to the politics of the other—whether that other is defined in terms of race, gender, species, or technology. She focuses on the metaphors which science uses and how those metaphors subtly determine the networks of power that control our world. The old traditional distance between people and machines has become harder to maintain and our assumptions about the clear distinction between human beings and machines collapse. The fact that disembodied relationship can feel as deep and intimate as face-to-face embodied ones is a shocking revelation undermining our common belief that only what we can touch, smell and taste is real. We discussed this issue at length in Chapter Four.

d.   The multi-self—we usually see ourselves as bound by our boundaries, identity, physical features, gender, etc. Our personal, professional, religious, and ethnic identity seems like something fixed, unchangeable, and unquestionable. The Internet shows us that our self-definition is a matter of self-decision and interpersonal agreement. The fact that I can introduce myself as a male while biologically I am a woman, or write as an adult when outside Cyberspace I am an adolescent, or pretend to be a religious Jew while holding atheist beliefs, is much more than deception. Relationships over the net are potentially identity transforming relationships. What we find out is that we have more control than we have ever imagined around constructing our identities. These experiences on the Internet can only be understood as part of a larger cultural context. It is the context of the post-modernist era, with its eroding boundaries between the real and the virtual, the animate and the inanimate, the unitary and the multiple self (Haraway, 1985; Turkle, 1995).

e. The Internet is "for free"—from its inception, Cyberspace became an environment where generosity prevails. Freeware (software distributed for free) and shareware (software that can be used after paying a small amount for registration) became common. One could find the most advanced word processors and spread-sheet programmes for free on the Internet. It seems as if people enjoyed sharing their creative products with others whom they have never met and mostly with whom they had no other connection whatsoever. This strange generosity, uncommon in most Western industrial societies, manifests itself in Internet forums too. Request for information or for assistance coming from forum members are usually answered quickly and with a lot of good will. Total strangers will give up hours of their time to send one another research data. In my field of expertise, group-psychotherapy, I could spend time looking for references in response to requests from people I have never heard of.

Behind this assumption lies the question of whether the virtual environment is going to be a capitalistic society or a utopian socialist one. There is a paradox between the so many Internet uses common for a capitalistic society (from commerce to bank-ing) and its so many communitarian uses (from support groups to connecting communities).

f. The Internet connects/disconnects people: for each of these two assumptions we can find evidence. It is true that time spent online is inevitably time we could have spent with others in our physical surroundings. We can also say that the connection to distant others is a form of detachment in itself (Turkle's book from 2011 is titled *Alone Together*). On the other hand we cannot ignore the fact that the Internet connects people from different cultures, countries, and ethnic origin. So the conclusion is that both are true: although the Internet is bringing us together, it also keeps us apart. The question is how we use it. In point of fact, this is the main subject of this book.

Disavowals: intimacy or E-ntimacy©?

In Chapter Six we saw that Internet forums are actually large groups. Participants in the large group usually look for the intimacy they are used to in small groups—and become disappointed. The large group is not capable of creating the warm-accepting-containing atmosphere that is easily built up in a small group. On the contrary, the large group is usually characterised by lack of face-to-face and mirroring interactions. Sometimes, both in large groups and online, we look for intimacy, hoping for compassion, yet often get the cruelty of strangers. As written in the introduction to my co-edited book about the large group (Weinberg & Schneider, 2003), this, in effect, categorises the dynamic understanding of the large group: such large numbers do not allow for intimacy but rather can engender feelings of difference and alienation. The crowd is not the place to establish close relationship with people. A typical short vignette from a large group of school psychologists, hinting to the search for intimacy:

> someone hesitated whether to share with the group what she wanted to talk about, and when "seduced" by other member, she suggested talking about love. She was sneered at verbally following her suggestion.

Popular wisdom describes intimacy as "into-me-you-see". If we look for this kind of intimacy in the large group we are sure to become frustrated and disappointed. But maybe another kind of intimacy is possible; an intimacy based on belonging, confluence, and influence? Surely, this is not the intimacy praised by the "let's talk about it" Western cultural norms and Hollywood movies. Neither is it the deep feeling of close encounters evoked by Buberian I–Thou relationship. It is more the feeling of togetherness, being a part of a community. Turkle (2011) points out that traditionally, the development of intimacy required privacy. Clearly, privacy is not available in Cyberspace, so we should rethink intimacy in new ways: "Intimacy without privacy reinvents what intimacy means" (p. 171).

On Internet large groups (forums), intimacy is usually based on the creation and development of a core group that carries on group norms of tolerance and openness, and an atmosphere of cohesion, "we-ness", and belonging. The core group consists of members that are more involved in the exchange of messages, post more often and become more salient and important in this virtual large group. Sometimes this togetherness moves to its extreme manifestation of the fourth basic assumption of one-ness (Turquet, 1974), where the individual merges with the crowd, losing his identity (the massification pole in Hopper's (1997) assumption), being endangered by a non-verbal mimetic engulfment mirroring (see Weinberg & Toder, 2004). When this kind of togetherness prevails, the large group massifies and a denial of differences appears creating the illusion of uniformity (Kernberg, 1989).

This is exactly what happens in Cyberspace. The fantasy of "we are all the same" in this virtual environment is very strong. Anonymity on the Internet enhances this fantasy because it seems as if there are no presumptions about the writer based on colour, age, or even gender. Even in forums based on professional interest (such as my group-psychotherapy discussion list, see Chapter Six) it seems at first that generally the voice of the junior, young, and inexperienced has the same weight and is heard just the same as the voice of the senior expert. The Internet seems to replicate the ideal flattened hierarchy suitable for post-modern global organisations. The reality on the Internet is different, which hints to a common denial and disavowal of differences. Although it seems that equal space and opportunity is given to both young and older, experienced and junior, very quickly the old differentiation (and sometimes discrimination) takes over. Playing with selves is a nice game, but as this game lasts, older identities emerge, as people bring their self-image and status into Internet communication.

As mentioned above, one of the major criticisms of outsiders who do not belong to Internet forums and community is in relation to intimacy. The assertion is: "Relations on the Internet cannot be real relationships with real intimacy." However, anonymity online—which can have the negative effects of de-individuation and alienation—can have positive effects too. McKenna and Green (2002) mention that anonymity on the Internet helps members express how they really feel and think, and encourages the emergence of healthy group norms.

We can also say that the quest for intimacy in Cyberspace denies the fact that on the Internet another kind of intimacy develops, for which I coin the term E-ntimacy©. This E-ntimacy© is based on fantasy and idealisation. It is a deep relationship between two (or more) non-bodies. But whereas Freud and classical psychoanalysis saw fantasy as opposed to and clouding reality, post-Freudian psychoanalytic authors (especially inter-subjective and relational ones; see Aron, 1996; Mitchell, 2002) regard fantasy as enriching and enhancing reality. And whereas idealisation has been considered as a dangerous illusion, inimical to stable long-term relationship, it can also be regarded as a process of bringing alive features of the other that are hidden and masked in ordinary interactions (Mitchell, 2002). In every era, certain ways of relating come to feel natural. In our time, the need to continuously be in touch, always connected to Cyberspace, does not in itself seem problematic or pathological. Similarly, on the Internet, a person's playing with multiple selves (Turkle, 1995)—which holds the possibility of exploring deeper layers of the selves beyond those bound to reality testing—meets well with the fantasy of the other, as long as both members in this bonding remember that Internet rules are different from face-to-face rules. The problem starts when people forget that Cyberspace is not a day-to-day space and try to enforce Internet rules on the reality outside, confusing intimacy and E-ntimacy©.

Social defences

Projection is the most obvious defence mechanism on the web. It is used massively, probably because we only have text data and no other cues. The lack of facial expression, tone of the voice, or any other embodied expression leaves the reader with many gaps in information s/he is trying to fill. Projection on the Internet leads to many misunderstandings and therefore conflicts. People interpret written text according to their fantasy and their own perception of the world, and not according to the author's world. True, it can happen outside Cyberspace too, but when we have other clues to the speaker's intention, such as the tone of her voice or his smile, misperceptions are minimised or more easily worked through. In face-to-face interaction people rely on the combination of textual, visual, and auditory cues to interpret the meaning of the speaker's sentences. This is so common that people do not notice how important each of these dimensions is to (what they think is) an exact understanding of the speaker. The Internet leaves the written word as the only source of interpretation and this leads to many misunderstandings. Suler (1996) writes that because the experience of the other person often is limited to text, there is a tendency for the user to project a variety of wishes, fantasies, and fears on to the ambiguous figure at the other end of Cyberspace.

Usually projections lead to a negative interpretation of the writer's intention, and might start word-wars ("flaming") when a comment that was meant to be humorous is conceived as insulting by the reader. But projections can also lead to idealisation. At other times the reader projects benevolent intentions upon the author, and develops idealised fantasies. It might be related to the current needs of the reader and to the written text that fits these needs. Idealisation on the Internet can be very strong, leading to infatuation and virtual romances on the one hand and to leaders' idealisation on the other.

The shift between negative projections and idealisations can create splits, when some objects are perceived as "all good", while other are perceived as "all bad". These poles are evident when conflicts in Internet forums arise, splitting the members into two parties, causing "flame wars" and the discharge of crude aggression. This is one of the possible dangerous dynamics of a large group, and the virtual large group is no exception (Weinberg, 2003b).

Structural oppression

At first glance it seems as if the Internet is providing an equal opportunity environment. There is no discrimination on the basis of colour, gender, or ethnics. Everyone is welcome to write whatever is in his or her mind. It is the most egalitarian society because social status does not pertain and the same space is given for the black and the white, the Jew or the Moslem, men and women, the rich and the poor, young and old, expert and novice. Cyberspace seems to eliminate differences and inequality.

If we examine the use of the Internet distribution by gender, for example, we will find out that there is still a difference between modern countries to traditional ones in this matter: in 2009, male and female Internet users in the USA were almost equally spread. However, in Morocco, while seventy-five per cent of the men used the Internet, only fifty per cent of the women did (www.itu.int/ITU-D/ict/statistics/Gender/). A significant gender bias towards men still exists in the adoption of modern information and communications technologies in less developed countries.

The same illusion exists regarding the use of the Internet all over the world. Theoretically it is the World Wide Web, but practically in poor countries many people cannot access the Internet either because the cost of computers and Internet connection is too high for their income, or because no service provider is available. In the Democratic

Republic of Congo, a poor country in Africa with a population of sixty-eight million people there are only 290,000 Internet users (0.45%), while in North America there were around 230 million Internet users in 2008 (news.bbc.co.uk/2/hi/technology/8552410.stm). Talking about globalisation and the "global village" in regard to the Internet is ignoring the fact that the growth of the Internet has been anything but even, and large areas of the world have scarcely been touched by the internet explosion. The barriers to technological development are exactly the same as the barriers to any economic development: market restrictions, lack of contract law, state controls, customs duties, bureaucracy, corruption, and so on. With these barriers still in place, diverting resources to information and communications technologies is just another distraction from other real structural differences.

A stable society develops where there is some assumed general agreement between its members or where a set of values can be identified which define the limits of both the social order and of individual contributions to social groups within that society. Most conventional territorial societies exhibit a hierarchical structure between the governed and the government, and power is exercised within certain constraints, which are usually imposed by the government and related to its ideology. In Cyberspace, a hidden structural hierarchy that resides in the Internet unconscious replaces the governmental ideology of established states. This structural oppression, with its inequality (related for example to gender and the distribution of financial resources) is well disguised under the common Internet illusion of "we are all the same".

As said earlier, the basic assumption of "one-ness" (Turquet, 1974) is ubiquitous in Cyberspace, and is responsible for this illusion of equality and equity. It is interesting that at the same time, in other Internet communities, the opposite assumption of "me-ness" (Lawrence, Bain, & Gould, 1996) can work as well, when people forget or choose to ignore that on the other side of the screen there are other human beings too, indulging in destructive acts, from sending viruses to becoming verbally abusive.

Collective memory

The Social unconscious of people belonging to a particular society can be co-constructed by collective memories. In fact, those collective memories, transferred from one generation to another, repeated through the public discourse or the written and electronic media, and iterated by leaders and citizens, create the communicational web of the foundation matrix that stands behind the social unconscious. The collective memories might be considered properties of the social unconscious. What is a collective memory and where does it reside?

The term collective memory was coined by Halbwachs (1980). It refers to the shared pool of information held in the memories of two or more members of a group. Collective memory can be shared, passed on and constructed by small and large groups. "A 'collective memory', as a set of ideas, images, feelings about the past, is best located not in the minds of individuals, but in the resources they share. There is no reason to privilege one form of resource over another—for example, to see history books as important but popular movies as not." (Irwin-Zarecka, 1994).

Notice that although we are talking about memory, which we usually expect to reside in the mind, or even in the brain of people, it is actually stored in a space that people share, which is the same as in the social unconscious case. It is clearly not the product of one person or one mind, but the result of the interaction of people's minds. "Yet collective memory is more than just an aggregate of individuals' personal memories, and such inevitably personal relief maps cannot possibly capture what an entire nation, for example, *collectively* considers historically eventful or uneventful" (Zerubavel, 2003, p. 28).

Collective memory can account for the vertical axis of the social unconscious. In fact, just as the social unconscious is the result of human interactions and relationships, but impacts the behaviour of individuals living in a specific society, collective memory shows similar confusing features, being co-constructed by the many, but showing itself in the memory of a person: "While the collective memory endures and draws strength from its base in a coherent body of people, it is individuals as group members who remember." (Halbwachs, 1980, p. 48).

However, it is unclear what collective memories people share nowadays. Not long ago people listened to one radio station or watched the same TV show, thus creating a common ground, joint values and shared memories. In the diverse society of today, with the many sources of available information, collective memories are gone (the exception is memories about community wide social trauma: as said before social traumas are very important in the construction of the social unconscious). As shown throughout this book, the Internet makes it even more confusing and paradoxical: On the one hand people are fed with information by so many Internet websites and resources that it is hard to speak of a common ground. On the other hand, the existence of social networks, and the ability to spread information by viral communication does guarantee that people's minds are influenced by the same resources and that they might have similar memories, creating the matrix for the Internet unconscious. This unconscious seems to be beyond specific geographical boundaries.

Internet and multiculturalism

There is no better place to gain perspective on our own cultural assumptions than on the Internet. Without moving from the chair, a person meets with people from all over the world, exchanging ideas, entering conflicts, creating E-ntimacy© with them. From a cultural awareness perspective, the Internet has been both an advantage and a liability. For people who are interested in other cultures it provides a significant amount of information and an interactivity that would be unavailable otherwise. However, for people who are not interested in other cultures there is some evidence indicating that the Internet enables them to avoid contact to a greater degree than ever before (another Internet paradox) because users can choose to largely interact with people similar to themselves. Cyberspace creates the opportunity of grasping the social construction of experiences we unthinkingly regard as universal and through that builds a path to one's own social unconscious. This encounter evokes a surprising clash between our presuppositions and those of other cultures. We can say that the Internet is the ultimate multi-culture.

Multi-culture is a term currently in vogue. Multiculturalism is defined as a situation where different cultures exist one beside the other (Leonetti, 1992). Differences between social and ethnic groups are very concrete and deep. The division into "us and them" (Berman, Berger, & Gutmann, 2000) is very basic and is built gradually for years, strengthened by education and social pressures. Oldenquist (1988) argues that human beings need social identities as entities, because otherwise they will feel isolated, alienated, and meaningless.

Multi-cultural societies are the norm nowadays, from Europe to the US. These societies face repeating problems of intolerance, difficulty with accepting "the other", and minority violence. A healthy society can contain many differences and diversities among people and social groups. In such a society there is place for different attitudes, opinions, norms, and behaviours as long as they do not enforce themselves on others. For this reason, the Internet seems an ideal society. Cyberspace is open to everyone, and one feels free to express any idea without censorship. As dialogue is disembodied there is no danger of activating physical force threatening to prevent people from expressing their opinions. But Cyberspace can be a dangerous psychological space. It is a place where impulsivity can win, aggression might prevail, verbal flaming can burst out, and regression takes over. In Cyberspace psychological vulnerabilities heighten because of the illusion of intimacy and due to the fact that one's voice can disappear in the void.

As both contradictory aspects are possible on the Internet, it can become a laboratory for exploring the conditions in which an authentic dialogue develops, and those in which destructive conflicts between social subgroups arise. When does freedom to express anything in Cyberspace become freedom to let out aggression and impulsivity? How can we avoid unfruitful ethnic clashes and intercultural tensions from developing on the Internet? As mentioned before, Holland (1996) saw the uncontrolled aggression expressed in Internet communication as one sign of the Internet regression and traced it to unconscious fantasies people have to the computer itself. Internet users tend to confuse humans and the machine. They are ready to hurt other participants in the discussion because the others are anonymous and unknown. So when they verbally abuse their dialogue partner, it does not look to them as if they hurt another human being, but more like playing with a machine or a video game. This means that one of the conditions (either on the Internet, face-to-face interaction, or social communication) is to "humanise the other". This can be done in many ways: from enhancing personal acquaintance to adding individual features that make the other less anonymous. We can see the impact of anonymity in large groups where it leads to alienation and massification/aggregation.

Another main factor impacting the atmosphere in an Internet forum is the leader's attitude and presence. A leader supporting tolerance, acceptance, and pluralism encourages an atmosphere of multicultural-ism. In Chapter Five we focused on some of the leader's functions and their implications for social leaders. The containing and protective functions are crucial for strengthening a multicultural approach. These functions are especially important in times of conflicts, crises, and frag-mentation. When Hopper's (1997) fourth basic assumption is evident in the group, the leader should be able to unify the fragments that are the result of aggregation or make room for diversity when encounter-ing massification. The issue of the Internet and multiculturalism might be a good field for quantitative research of different leadership styles.

Conclusions and implications

Our long journey led us from group analysis to the Internet uncon-scious. We have started with introducing the frame of reference of group analysis (Chapter Two) finding out that group analysis can be used to explore and understand larger groups and societal processes, providing tools to analyse unconscious processes and learn about culture and communities including the Internet culture. Is there Internet culture?; something more substantial than shared mastery of the e-mail or chatroom "smiley," or is that an oxymoron?

Understanding society and the Internet through its unconscious elements adds new dimensions to scientific exploration. When using the group analytic frame of reference for studying a specific social unconscious, one goes beyond the visible elements and discovers unknown powerful discourses existing in the culture under scrutiny. There are more practical implications in this exploration regarding leadership, multicultural societies, and large group processes.

Cyberspace, which became an arena for social experience, invol-untarily reveals crucial aspects of identity such as gender, age, and race. Usually these bits of identity are completely masked by computer-mediated communications. Studying the Internet uncon-scious reveals that what at first seem like binary relationships (person/machine, fantasy/reality, physical/ethereal states) includes a space between binaries. Examining groups and relationship on the Internet thus has many implications for daily life.

Cyberspace is a place to explore utopian possibilities, but also a junk yard for traditional culture. When impacted by the utopian view of the Internet I was fascinated by this new postmodernist playground and the possibility of exploring unconscious features of our culture through using group analysis. Shifting to the other extreme of the dystopian view, I was disappointed to find out that when immigrating to Cyberspace, people could not leave behind their drives, needs, and perceptions of the other and that the same, socially constructed reality exists in this disembodied environment. Both extremes are probably equally true.

Turkle (1995, p. 139) pointed out that there is a parallel between the historical development of psychoanalysis and historical development of artificial intelligence:

> In both fields there has been movement away from a model in which a few structures act on more passive substance. Psychoanalysis began with drive and artificial intelligence began with logic. Both moved from a centralized to a decentred model of mind. Both moved towards a metatheory based on objects and emergence.

We will greatly benefit if, instead of resisting this parallel between psychoanalysis and artificial intelligence, human and machine, face-to-face and virtual interaction, we explore and learn from these parallels about our culture.

"Psychoanalysis is about what two people can say to each other if they agree not to have sex" (Bersani & Phillips, 2008, p. 1). The psychoanalytic/psychotherapeutic setting allows for an intimacy that is not exactly the same as the intimacy created when two people are not bound to the therapeutic rules. *E-ntimacy© is about what people can say to each other if they agree not to have a body.* It is not an impersonal intimacy: it is a different kind of intimacy. In fact, Internet E-ntimacy© challenges the Western cultural norms of independence, as the always-on connection is sensed as a more collaborative self. As Turkle (2011) put it, "we are together even when we are alone" (p. 169).

CHAPTER EIGHT

Yalom's therapeutic factors virtually examined

(This chapter was written in collaboration with Ravit Raufman)

Yalom's factors

Since Irvin Yalom (1970) described the therapeutic factors functioning in every psychotherapy group, these factors appear in any textbook about group psychotherapy. It is impossible to discuss group therapy, or groups in general, without considering them, examining their emergence and function in the specific group. In the latest edition of their book, Yalom & Leszcz (2005) discussed the essence of successful group therapy and proposed a list of eleven elementary factors of therapeutic change. Table 1 describes thirteen therapeutic factors according to the American Group Psychotherapy Association.

As noted by Yalom, not all factors are always present or equally important in every group. There is substantial variance among groups and group leaders in the emphasis they put on each of these factors. Thus, in some groups (e.g., Yalom-type groups) there is more emphasis on interpersonal learning, while other groups emphasise imparting information (for example, psycho-educational groups). Furthermore, group participants may differ in how much they are able to profit from each factor. For example, one participant could experience the imitative behaviour as being most important, while for another the

Table 1: The therapeutic factors (Yalom & Leszcz, 2005)

Therapeutic Factors	*Definition*
Universality	Members recognise that other members share similar feelings, thoughts, and problems
Altruism	Members gain a boost to self concept through extending help to other group members
Instillation of hope	Member recognises that other members' success can be helpful and they develop optimism for their own improvement
Imparting information	Education or advice provided by the therapist or group members
Corrective recapitulation of primary family experience	Opportunity to re-enact critical family dynamics with group members in a corrective manner
Development of socialising techniques	The group provides members with an environment that fosters adaptive and effective communication
Imitative behaviour	Members expand their personal knowledge and skills through the observation of group members' self-exploration, working through, and personal development
Cohesiveness	Feelings of trust, belonging, and togetherness experienced by the group members
Existential factors	Members accept responsibility for life decisions
Catharsis	Members release of strong feelings about past or present experiences
Interpersonal learning-input	Members gain personal insight about their inter personal impact through feedback provided from other members
Interpersonal learning-output	Members provide an environment that allows members to interact in a more adaptive manner
Self-understanding	Members gain insight into psychological motiva tion underlying behaviour and emotional reactions

Source: Copied from the AGPA website at www.agpa.org/guidelines/ factorsandmechanisms.html

strongest therapeutic factor could be instillation of hope. The distinction between these factors is arbitrary, and the factors are interdependent and cannot be dealt with separately.

What do we know about these factors in relation to groups existing in Cyberspace? How much we can deduce from their efficacy in face-to-face groups and apply them to groups that are "virtual"? To what extent does the uniqueness of Cyberspace require reframing or re-evaluation of these factors, as part of renaming and re-examining many other phenomena related to groups on the Internet?

To enliven our exploration metaphorically, let us recall a famous fable: "The blind men and the elephant". Six blind men were asked to determine what an elephant looked like by feeling different parts of its body. The blind man who had felt the tail said that the elephant is like a rope; the one who felt the leg said the elephant is like a pillar; the one who felt the belly said the elephant is like a wall; the one who felt the trunk said the elephant is like a tree branch; the one who felt the ear said the elephant is like a hand fan; and the one who felt the tusk said the elephant is like a solid pipe. They continued to passionately argue, trying to convince one another, eventually unable to determine what form an elephant has. However, even if their blindness did not allow them to reach a final conclusion, it inflamed their hot debate and consolidated the blind men as a group. The moral of this story is to question whether there is only one correct way to determine how an elephant (or the world) looks like, and whether people who have different belief systems can establish a group discourse to reach harmony. It goes without saying that when discussing groups on the Internet the question of blindness is even more relevant.

Research on the therapeutic factors on the Internet

In fact, there is a paucity of research activity about Yalom's therapeutic factors on the Internet. In a pilot study of a computer support group for six women with breast cancer, Weinberg, Uken, Schmale, and Adamek (1995) researched the therapeutic factors of instillation of hope, universality, group cohesion, catharsis, and altruism. Results indicated that participants in the group perceived these factors to be present, with the factors of instillation of hope, group cohesion, and universality viewed as most prevalent. Salem, Bogat, and Reid (1997) identified two helping processes on Internet groups: helping others (i.e., altruism) and advice or information exchanged (i.e., imparting information). In another study about online users coping with disabilities, Finn (1999) evaluated data with a content analysis and found evidence that five of Yalom's eleven elements of therapeutic factors operated in online support groups: catharsis, universality, group cohesion, the providing of information (i.e., imparting of information), and of taking on the "helper role" (i.e., altruism).

Liebert, Smith-Adcock, and Munson (2008) found the factors of universality, catharsis, instillation of hope, imparting information, and altruism to be helpful in Internet support groups. Four of the five factors, universality (Finn, 1999), catharsis (Perron, 2002), and in different terms, imparting information and altruism (Salem, Bogat, & Reid, 1997) have been reported in previous studies, providing credence to the findings in their study. Universality was the most frequently reported of these five factors. Partial evidence was found for a sixth therapeutic process, cohesiveness, in their investigation. A later study conducted by Barak (2007), who wrote several articles about Internet self-help groups, found that therapeutic factors such as group cohesiveness, catharsis, leadership, disclosure, and advice, clearly emerge in an online group's activity.

Yalom's factors available on the Internet

Let us start with the factor of *hope*. Many times hope starts by clarifying the expectations of group members. In contrast to groups that exist in a joint physical space in which pre-screening of group members is possible and the instillation of hope starts even before the group begins, this is impossible in groups on the Internet. As mentioned in Chapter Six, the contract in Internet forums is very loose. However, in Cyberspace a powerful potential exists, closely related to the concept of hope. The possibility of expanding oneself beyond time and space limitations, rising above the restrictions of physical existence to create a disembodied interaction, and allowing an experience that crosses boundaries are very hopeful experiences in themselves. Here is an example of one of the writer's (Raufman) personal experiences:

> As a mother of young children one of the main dilemmas I had to deal with daily was the gap between the wish to develop professionally and the demands of raising children and household, both requiring

physical presence. Probably most mothers raising the children know this experience, accompanied with the never ending feeling that there is not enough time and that leaving the house physically involves a high price. Conferences and professional meetings in my country and around the world remained wishful thinking, an unactualised reminder in the calendar. The entrance of the Internet to my daily routine brought a revolution, and was very meaningful for me and for other mothers, suddenly enabling communication with the entire world without leaving home. One day I found a website designated for a clinical psychologist and other psychotherapists, composed of many forums dealing with different psychological topics. For me it was the beginning of the new era: after spending a whole night exploring the new virtual spaces, I signed up for a forum of psychotherapists involved with arts (writing, painting, taking pictures, etc.). From that moment my life changed. I could not foresee how much this virtual group would become a significant part of my daily life, of my psyche, and other aspects of my life. I will bring more examples from this group later, but as for hope, the new possibility of joining the group without time and space boundaries gave me a lot of hope.

Another example is taken from a website dedicated to incest survivor women. This website included many blogs of these women. In a research conducted by Raufman and Milo (in press) it was found that one of the most powerful aspects of these blogs was that some of the women told their sad, horrible personal narratives for the first time there. Simply by talking about their continuing traumatic experiencing, until then a concealed secret, the ability to disclose their story using artistic ways of expression (drawing, pictures), under the cover of a disguised identity which created a sense of safety, gave these bloggers a feeling of hope that was therapeutic in itself. It seems that the instillation of hope in this example has to do with the same feeling of elation mentioned before, related to the ability of rising beyond the limitations of time and space, and even beyond the physical existence of the human body. The bloggers left their stories on the Internet in perpetuity. This elation does not originate only from the practical dimensions of voice and witness but also from the painful recognition about the fragility of human existence: that is, an awareness of the limitations of our physical mortality is deeply connected to our fear of death. Writing a blog on the Internet reminds us that the psyche is eternal and infinite, in contrast to the human body, which is limited and mortal. We can definitely say that all the above is related to Yalom's *existential factors*. These factors clearly exist also in support groups, abundant on the Internet, for potentially terminal illnesses such as cancer and AIDS.

Talking about blogs brings us to a related subject of online confessional sites, on which people log on anonymously and post a confession or a secret (for example www.postsecret.com). Because the writers do not know who reads their confessions, it seems as if all they want is to vent. Confessing to a website is like getting something "out", and is based on the assumption that bad feelings become less toxic when released. This is actually similar to *catharsis* or getting things off your chest included in the therapeutic factors. Turkle (2011), who interviewed people posting these confessions, found out that some of them satisfy needs for feeling better after confessing to the website, but it does not lead to talking to those they wronged or trying to make amends. It is an interesting question whether catharsis in itself is therapeutic in the sense that it makes people simply feel better, or whether it helps people make some behavioural change and ask for people's forgiveness when they feel guilty.

The *cathartic* factor surely works in discussion lists where people not only confess to a faceless screen, but also interact with others after expressing their emotions. Remember the exchange of e-mails on the group psychotherapy list, described in Chapter Six, when a forum member expressed his broken heart after losing his newborn son. I repeat his message here because it depicts so well the intense emotions accompanying catharsis:

> My heart is broken—words can't convey the grief, and I realize only now that the depth of this pain is beyond comprehension. I feel waves of horrible sadness and utter bewilderment. I'm sure that anger will come, though it has not yet shown itself. (Personal communication, group psychotherapy discussion list, 2 July 2000)

In this case the cathartic effect seems to amplify following the resonance his words created in other people's hearts and with their empathic responses. We should remember that sometimes, when we share our burden, other people, especially on the Internet due to anonymity—may use our vulnerability for their own purposes. People tell their sad stories hoping to be paid with empathy. On the

Internet authenticity depends on the cohesion and atmosphere developed on the specific forum.

Yalom and Leszcz (2005) mention that the therapeutic factors are not disconnected from one another and many times work together. If we go back to the blogs of incest survivors, it seems that the factor of *hope* was closely connected to other factors such as *universality* and *altruism*. In contrast to the hostile, humiliating, and insensitive attitude they had received—not only from their perpetrators but also from their family members—on the Internet the bloggers/survivors received a different attitude—warm, respectful, and understanding, or at least listening. This attitude went beyond expressions of support, and clearly manifested the factor of universality: "I know what you're talking about. I went through the same thing." The participants felt the need, or even the responsibility, to stand by the trauma sister's side, and to create a new world in which altruism replaces abuse, alienation turns into support, and from the depths of despair opens a door of hope. In turn, the empathic respondents receive the gift of experiencing their own efficacy, which in turn strengthens their felt sense of personal power and agency. It is a reciprocal process

Remember that *universality* is especially important in sexual abuse groups, and on the Internet it might even have a stronger potential and impact. Because the Internet crosses country and continental boundaries, the feeling of the writer, especially when people respond from all over the world, is that his or her own unique experience is shared by people from diverse cultures and geographical places. Relating to the forum for the sexually abused women, many of them openly expressed their feeling that for the first time they are not alone. For years they felt guilty, shameful, lonely, and kept the secret to themselves. On that website they found not only a listening ear and a supportive hand, but also responses shattering the myth that they are abnormal and that "something is wrong with them", or that they are guilty of what has happened to them. The women on the website responded to one another in powerful and touching ways, sharing their personal stories in detail, contributing to the continuous effort to understand and reframe the abusive events, and also providing useful details about coping, from legal issues to advice about establishing a connection with a new partner in the shade of trauma. Although some of them might have heard this advice from other sources (e.g., welfare agents, therapists, professional literature about abuse, media), nothing can be compared to advice coming from the mouth of a woman that went through the same horrors.

The above is a good example of the *imparting information* factor. The women who went through abuse shared and updated one another with information about the option of suing their abusers, and to fully grasp that what they went through was deviant and abnormal. Women who have already revealed their secret outside the forum shared with their "sisters" the consequences of this dramatic act and encouraged them to do the same. A special folder on that website is titled "useful information" in which theoretical and practical materials could be found, including statistical data, description of the PTSD (post-traumatic stress disorder) syndrome and possible consequences of sexual abuse such as dissociative identity disorder, plus links to other relevant pages.

Another example for the meaning of *imparting information* on the Internet is taken from a research project exploring folklore products in Cyberspace (Raufman & Ben-Cnaan, 2009). As part of that project, the researchers explored a unique version of the "Little Red Riding Hood" fairy tale that appeared on the Internet. The version discussed appeared on 26 June 2006, on one of the Israeli Channel 7's forums, a nationalist-religious channel. The forum is called *"Torath Haim b'Oz"* (www.inn.co.il/Forum/lmf_read.aspx/11795), and is geared towards teenagers belonging to the "Ariel" youth movement, a nationalist-religious youth group. "Ariel" is a splinter group, which began as part of the religious-Zionist movement "Bnei Akiva", and is a more orthodox movement. Activities between boys and girls, for example, are conducted separately, for the sake of modesty. Before we turn into the analysis of the fairy tale, we focus on the way that forum members helped one another in daily issues.

Many of the issues discussed on that forum included practical questions, reflecting the confusion of the religious youngsters in a modern society. Typical questions were raised inquiring whether a specific activity as permitted according to the Halacha (religious) or Rabbinic law, with participants bringing citations from the Torah[1] and other resources or quoting famous Rabbis. It seems as if the participants saw one another as an easily available source of information about daily issues.

This is not new in Cyberspace, as we know about many and various forums that are dedicated to the distribution and exchange of information. Just think about forums that share cooking recipes and exchange useful advice in household issues, or forums for women who go through fertility treatments and share information about medical centres and procedures. There are thousands of forums of questions and answers about health, financial, politics, house decoration, child rearing, publishing books, legal advice, and any other issue that interests people. In addition to the information that is shared in all of these forums, there is a sense that we do not have to be alone and struggle with daily life just by ourselves. We are all "one human tissue (matrix)" and we can learn from the experience of others.

Within the context of the Ariel's forum discussions, we can see how the Red Riding Hood story reflects the preoccupation of the members with moral, ethical, and practical themes, many of which are dedicated to examining the nature of boy–girl relationships, under headings, such as "What is permitted and what is forbidden". For example, one of the participants raises the following question: "If I go to Bnei Akiva and one of the boys says he wants to talk with me privately about something, what should I do? (I'm always trying to avoid him). What should I do, I need an answer right away [. . .]" (Personal communication, "*Torath Haim b'Oz*" discussion list 12 February 2007). In fact, the participant is asking: "How dangerous is it to talk to strange boys?"

The relationship between Red Riding Hood and the wolf, appearing in this Internet version, includes sexual, aggressive, and dichotomous content, as a story distinguishing between good and bad creatures, aggressors and victims, and perhaps between a frightening male and a seemingly innocent girl. Having an access to an Internet forum allows the examination of the participants' responses to the text, the relationship among the forum members, and even the relationship between the Ariel group and other youth movements to which they related in the forum. The Ariel members made use of the forum to strengthen their ideological identity's values and norms and enhance their sense of *cohesion*, especially important for adolescents. *Universality* was not only a factor revealed during participation in the forum, but also a factor deliberately created by members in order to intensify the common identity. For example, in one of the posts, a participant asked: "Who are we and how different are we from other groups?" The responses of the other members were quick and flooded the forum with subject lines suggesting a joint identity differentiating them from other groups.

As mentioned in Chapters Five and Six, the *cohesion* felt in an Internet forum is quite surprising, as we are talking of a large group with very loose boundaries, where people can easily sign off and membership is unstable. However, as explained in Chapter Six, the core group is responsible for the illusion of a cohesive small group. Getting back to the Red Riding Hood fairy tale appearing in the *"Torath Haim b'Oz"* forum, we can say that a fairy tale genre is the most universal of all literature genres. Although it can look like a funny text whose purpose is simply to entertain the participants, the volume of responses and their complexity hints to more ingredients involved. Fairy tales, as a genre that exists in different peoples, crossing cultural and historical spaces, known to everyone, establishes a common matrix, and can represent aspects related to the large group: the human species large group. Fairy tales can be recruited to strengthen norms of a specific culture and to transfer social/cultural messages. All these are done in templates that are stable along decades and cultures, having a universal status. The format of Little Red Riding Hood appearing in the above forum opened with:

> Once upon a time, in Jerusalem, the holy city,
> There lived Red Riding Hood, so little and pretty.
> With her righteous mama, and her father, thanks god,
> The head of a Yeshiva[2]—a man of his word.

This opening clarifies that, on the one hand we are talking about a well-known literature heroine, and a story known to everyone (thus enhancing universality not only among the forum members, but among the members of the imagined large group of human mankind), but on the other hand it is transformed and adjusted for a specific culture with its own codes, creating a subgroup inside the large group. This element is prominent in sentences emphasising religious aspects, shown in a parodic way in the story. For example:

> "Hasten, take the basket of sweets I have kept.
> Don't look so worried, its Kosher, of course
> Under the seal of the Highest Rabbinic Court".
> A book of Psalms took the virtuous lass,
> And rushed to her mother's bidding, at last.

Or, in another place, manifesting the height of the parody:

He remembered that he had drank milk earlier[3],
So he let pass a while, before devouring her.
Then he washed out his mouth, said grace over food[4],
And swallowed the woman-so poor and so good.

The writer of the text relies on the knowledge existing in the religious society so that the mentioning of one word evokes a complete system of associations and symbols. Using this assumption, it is enough to mention a few hints from the orthodox Jewish life to activate a similar association system at the members of the group: Here is another example:

"Why are your ears so big?" she asked painfully,
"To listen to Torah lessons", he answered piously.
"And why is your nose bent and crooked like that?"
"To smell fragrant spices at the nightfall of Sabbath"[5]
"And why are your teeth as big as caverns?" she asked again,
"To gobble you and say grace after the meal, Amen!"

The good ending(?) of this Internet religious version follows the genre rules and the universal template of the tale as well, while at the same time suggests a culturally dependent solution:

In a nearby Yeshiva, while prayers were said.
A young scholar heard the cries of the maid.
The youth with the side locks went straight ahead,
And opened the belly, rejoicing they weren't dead.
The village matchmaker was soon on the spot
And made a betrothal offer to the Red and the "big shot".
They lived happily ever since, praise the Lord,
And they have ten children, may there be many more, all blessed by God.

This unique and complicated version, and the way it functions as a social/cultural agent among the forum members, creates an elusive link between universal issues, with the need to belong and be immersed in them and at the same time to rebel against them. Moreover, between issues of establishing the identity of a group differentiating itself from other groups, by drawing its unique features, this unique version creates a different kind of universality: the universality within the small group.

The group *cohesiveness* enhanced through the communication in the forum is obvious, and especially relevant for teenagers who are in a stage where identification with peers assists in the crystallisation of a new identity, replacing the primary identification with parents and belonging to the family. *Interpersonal learning*, another therapeutic factor, exists in the experience of teenagers meeting on Cyberspace. Actually, it is especially relevant for ultra-orthodox religious Jews who are not allowed to use the Internet by some extreme Rabbis[6]. Surfing the Internet can be like Little Red Riding Hood's walking in the forest, with the danger of "diverting from the right road". The participants in the forum experience something forbidden, or at least socially dangerous, and are exposed to the dangers revealed through the Internet, within a closed society. At the same time they use the forum to strengthen the norms, values, and ethical codes of the religious culture.

Apparently, most of the participants in the forum are girls. In the Jewish orthodox conservative society, the modesty of females and the need to refrain from an inappropriate acquaintance with boys is of primary concern. This issue is at the centre of the fairy tale, and for the girls participating in the forum the narrative allows discussing this problematic dilemma, and also allows for talking with boys in a way that is impossible outside the Internet. Parallel themes exist in the forum under the title "should activities of boys and girls be separate", or in a post dealing with the question of how the girls could reach the women divided part of the synagogue without passing through the boys section, touching them inadvertently. Responses to these kinds of questions were many and it seems as if this issue is loaded with emotions.

Many researchers (e.g., Davies, 2006; Polak, 2006[7]) have dealt with the phenomenon of girls surfing the Internet and its meaning for their development. Other researchers (see Jones, 1997; Turkle, 2011) write about the meaning of the Internet for adolescents, intensively dealing with questions of identity. Perhaps like Little Red Riding Hood, and with exploration of the relationship between sexes, the Internet and all its possibilities can become exciting yet dangerous (as Red Riding Hood found out while establishing her relationship with the wolf). It is clear that for *"Torath Haim b'Oz"* forum members, using the forum is similar to strolling in Little Red Riding Hood's forest: will they be swallowed by the malicious wolf, or will they come out of this journey more mature and resilient? The above discussion shows that another factor Yalom mentions, *developing of socialising techniques*, is also involved in the intensive process of participating in the forum. As pointed out, it is through the discussion that the participants practice some abilities of interacting with the other sex and learn about how to behave in their community.

Cohesion or incohesion?

Although there is a lot of evidence, displayed above, for the existence of virtual groups' cohesion, we need to remember Hopper's fourth basic assumption of incohesion, mentioned several times throughout this book (e.g., Chapter Two), strongly prevailing in large groups. As Internet groups are large groups disguised as small groups (see Chapter Six) we can expect incohesion to occur in these groups as well.

> In an Internet forum of therapists from a certain State in the USA, existing for several years, that felt very cohesive and intimate, one of the participants suggested a face-to-face meeting. The forum was divided into two camps: Those who had felt excited about this opportunity to see their virtual friends and came to the meeting, and those who preferred to leave the relationship in the virtual space. Following this meeting, people who did not participate in it felt excluded, hurt and unheard, and those who did—felt misunderstood and attacked. The forum became more and more divided, conflicts frequently emerged in the discussions, and fragmentation crept into the group process. (The name of the forum has been omitted for reasons of confidentiality)

How do we understand this paradoxical result where the virtual group feels very cohesive and the insertion of a face-to-face meeting creates incohesion and fragmentation? It seems as if two perceptions of the Internet forum collided in this case: One focusing on the forum as providing a comfortable way to meet without the costs and trouble of travelling, time limitations, and commitment, etc., while the other perception emphasised the forum as a virtual space, with a unique potential, whose power is derived from its disembodied features. Many forum members experienced this virtual space as a kind of environment creating or increasing a "fantastic experience", allowing an encounter with parts of the self that are repressed or unexpressed in the "realistic" space. A face-to-face meeting was experienced as ruining this important fantasy. The potential of the Internet to blur the boundaries between reality and fantasy, body and mind, is perceived not only as increasing the potential for self-expression, but also as symbolising the freedom of the human spirit, unbounded by space and time, just like the virtual forum.

Factors not always available on the Internet

Is the *corrective recapitulation of primary family experience* also available on the Internet? At first glance it seems unlikely, but we might change our mind after reading the personal report of one of the authors of this chapter (Raufman) about her experience in the forum mentioned before of psychotherapists who are also involved in arts (which actually portrays additional factors such as *cohesion*):

> Very soon, and quite surprisingly, this forum became meaningful in my life. I found myself fantasising about interactions with the different participants, eagerly waiting for new posted messages, debating inside myself what I want to post and how to respond to others, and trying to resolve the powerful emotional experience related to this group. As a new forum member I introduced myself to the group, but with no response and no echo. It is difficult to know why it my introduction was unanswered in a virtual environment and, as mentioned in Chapter Six, the imaginary space is open to endless projections. For me, the experience was of a new child joining an already established family, whose older sisters and brothers are too busy to mentor the newbie into the group. This experience intensified due to the background of my family of origin, as I am the youngest of several sisters. However, the history of the virtual group can easily be retrieved from its previous communication. I found myself researching the past of the forum, reading previous posts and learning about the members, their relationships, the group climate, which posts are responded and which are ignored, etc. As time passed by, I found my way to belong to the group, express myself in a meaningful way, establishing my position in this new family. One day a new member appeared in the forum, introducing herself and presenting an art creation asking for a response. This group entrance was very different from mine, as I introduced myself hesitantly, not daring to present an art piece or asking for a response. The forum members were quick to respond to this newcomer, praising her art piece. For the first time in my life I had a "little sister", and even though we are talking about a virtual sister, the feelings of competition and envy were not virtual at all.

This self-report shows how family dynamics can easily be repeated and re-enacted in an Internet forum. The fact that the author did not know this newcomer or how she looked, had never met her, and only saw the few details that every forum members wrote in his/her identification card, increases our awareness that the virtual environment creates very concrete and real feelings among forum members. The un-embodied entity that is so typical of Cyberspace, and is so different from the embodied interaction we encounter in face-to-face groups, facilitated a strong connection with the author's inner feelings and allowed her to explore in depth her experience of envy and its origins. It enabled her to understand from a new perspective the feelings of her original family members when she entered their family. It felt like a strong experience, accompanied with the joy of self-revelation and creative playfulness, especially on the background of a forum that deals with arts, where members present stories, poems, pictures and drawings, discussing them creatively.

However, it seems that although Internet forums can recreate family dynamics, and it is clear from the above example that the primary family experience is part of processes that members of discussion lists go through, not always does it necessarily lead to a *corrective* recapitulation. Apparently, there are (at least) two possible ways to deal with the faceless forum and fill the gaps when family dynamics are enacted: either using projections, thus repeating the old experience and many times becoming hurt again if these dynamics are hurtful (sometimes, after using projection, even acting out the unresolved conflict), or turning inside and exploring the inner feelings, learning from the experience something valuable about oneself.

We assume that people choose between these options based on their personality and tendency for self-exploration of their use of projections. However, because the Internet is not a safe enough environment and there is no therapist who helps explore inner issues in discussion lists (certainly, this is not their task), most of the time the factor of the *corrective recapitulation of primary family experience* will not be easily available on the Internet (unless an interactively savvy participant plays this role without a therapist).

Unique therapeutic factors on the Internet

Weinberg and Weishut (2012), discussing Yalom's factors in large groups, identified some unique factors that are not mentioned by

Yalom, perhaps because they are usually rare in small groups and are more typical for the large group. In Chapter Six, Internet forums were described as large groups with an illusion of a small group. This calls for examining these factors that are more typical of a large group on Internet groups as well. The two factors that are available and prominent in the large group, but almost absent from the small group are the *representation of society* and *the struggle for power*.

Weinberg and Weishut (2012) argue that the *representation of society* as a therapeutic factor working in large groups may be considered as parallel to the *corrective recapitulation of the primary family* factor working in the small group. If this is the case in large groups, it certainly is in virtual groups. On the Internet, no less than in large groups, we can find a huge diversity of people from different national, cultural, and ethnic groups, religious backgrounds, gender, and age. Cyberspace offers exceptional possibilities for learning about the enormous diversity within society and one's own individual position. Thus, participation in an Internet forum enhances the feeling that the member is "a citizen of the world", enriched with interactions and connections with so many different interesting people, each coming from an unfamiliar culture. It goes without saying that such an opportunity to easily connect with this diversity and learn from so many peoples' different experiences could not exist before the Internet era.

The other additional factor mentioned by Weinberg and Weishut (2012) as unique to large groups, *the struggle for power*, can also be detected in the virtual environment, but to a lesser degree. As said before, there are many large group typical dynamics appearing in Internet forums: one of them is the fear of participants to express their voice and the narcissistic hurt when one finally writes something and one's voice seems to be lost in Cyberspace. It forces participants to struggle with the question of vulnerability and how much they are ready to risk feeling rejected and insignificant in the virtual crowd. Cyberspace provides a social environment that can become a good playground to exercise one's power and explore one's influence on community. The question that many people ask themselves in the large group: "Do I dare disturb the universe?" takes a more powerful form on the Internet, because this endless space is really perceived as "the universe". Belonging to Internet forums and discussion groups, being connected to people from faraway places, interacting with cultures to which I could only have dreamed about, creates a powerful feeling that "the world is at the tip of my finger". Participation in Internet forums can be empowering, helping one attain an inner level of self-assurance. Here is a quote of a college junior member, cited from Turkle's book (2011, p. 168): "I feel that I am part of a larger thing, the Net, the Web. The world. It becomes a thing to me, a thing I am part of. And the people, too, I stop seeing them as individuals, really. They are part of this larger thing."

Summary

A combination of Yalom's therapeutic factors, so important in small groups, exists on the Internet as well. Some of them (such as universality and hope) are even intensified in Cyberspace communities and Internet forums. Others (such as the corrective recapitulation of the family of origin) are less available on the Internet, depending on the participant's and specific group's ability to self-reflect.

Both research and personal experience clearly show that an Internet forum can become cohesive (usually through a core group), and that universality is a common factor in Cyberspace. People feel so strongly that they are not alone and that many identify with their situation. In fact, universality may feel even stronger on the Internet compared to face-to-face small groups, because the supportive and acknowledging responses of people from different countries and cultures strengthens the feeling that the writer is not alone and that his/her unique experience is shared by others. Universality unites people of diversity as they share similar thoughts, feelings, fears and/or reactions with their cyber community.

Catharsis, instillation of hope, imparting information, and altruism were also found in studies to be helpful in Internet support groups. Instillation of hope and existential factors are amplified on the Internet simply because it is perceived as an endless-timeless space. The ability to rise above the limitation of time and space is really stimulating and hope inspiring. In a subtle way this possibility in Cyberspace deals with one of the most basic existential anxieties, fear of death.

Most of Yalom's factors were described in this chapter as functioning on the Internet, improving people's well-being. The one factor that might not be working for everyone is the corrective recapitulation of the primary family. The original family dynamics might be activated and re-enacted, but it is left for the participant to make a corrective use of this occurrence, and it is possible that only people who use reflective thought can elaborate on these issues in Internet groups.

In addition to the well-known Yalom factors, other factors that are typical of the large group, such as representation of society and the struggle for power, also exist on the Internet, contributing to the ability of members to benefit from their experience in Internet communities. Online, we feel enhanced. Once we remove ourselves from our physical, untidy lives, we feel as if we have overcome some common human restrictions and limitations. The potential for growth, change, and social experimentation contribute to the group's cohesion and perceived helpfulness. Altogether, the Internet provides an exciting, powerful and unique space. Cyberspace is actually a huge transitional space (Winnicott, 1987) with boundless possibilities for people to play and experiment, fantasise and imagine: and that is why it embodies therapeutic potential.

Notes

1. Torah—the entire body of religious law and learning, including both sacred literature and oral tradition.
2. Yeshiva—religious Talmudic college.
3. Drank milk earlier—kosher foods that contain meat cannot be eaten with dairy.
4   Blessings over food—grace after meals
5. Fragrant spices on the eve of Sabbath—a Jewish ceremony involving the use of wine, spices, and candles at the conclusion of the Sabbath. Smelling the spices signifies the hope for a fragrant week; the light signifies the hope for a week of brightness and joy.
6. In the year 2000, a council of respected Torah scholars pronounced use of the Internet to be severely forbidden. Despite this, it was considered important to pose a specific restriction on Haredic teenagers not to use the Internet. Today, there are many Haredic websites that make use of modern technology for their own internal discussions, despite the rabbinical restrictions regarding Internet use that is not work-oriented. In fact, many Haredic families do use home computers and the Internet for political, social, religious, and commercial purposes, as a result of technological assimilation and compatibility with the community's cultural

structure (for additional reading, see 9.10.03, www.ynet.co.il–a review of Barzilai, 2003).

7.   Polak shows that Internet sites geared towards girls focus on subjects such as sexual maturation and development. This allows girls to discover themselves via dialogs and discussions with other girls (Polak 2006). Davies (2006) claims that young girls demand their rightful place in society through participating in Internet communities.

Conclusion

The Internet is a huge potential space, the ultimate playground in which people can creatively work through the basic human dilemmas that accompany any relationship, group or society. By examining the playground of Internet forums we can explore these dilemmas and the conflicts among a variety of needs. Throughout this book I identified and explored these dilemmas and conflictual needs, discussing their paradoxes in Cyberspace, as the Internet allows for solutions that are different than in face-to-face relationship and groups. Most of the time these solutions creatively involve a win/win (both/and) strategy, instead of an either/or (all or none).

Following are the main issues and paradoxes regarding group participation and intimate relationships as seen in groups on the Internet. Described and analysed throughout the book, these are presented together with the main conclusions:

- *Level of commitment*: participating in an online group allows for regulation of the level of involvement and commitment in relationship. In contrast to face-to-face groups, where people are expected to keep about the same amount of emotional investment over time, in online groups participants can maintain periods of strong involvement while at other times (either because of the pressures of daily life, lack of time, or emotional overload) be less involved and withdraw to a more observing position. This ebb and flow of involvement in a group or relationship is normative and acceptable in Internet connection.

- *Dependency* vs. *independence*: online, people can handle better the dilemma of dependency/independence or the fear of losing their freedom and being engulfed by relationship, *vs.* being totally independent but isolated. This is the conflict between the need to surrender to the other and the need to experience oneself as an independent agent who is masterful and in control. Internet groups help us not to lose sight of the need we all have to surrender—to have the experience that it is not all up to us, and that there is some benevolent force outside of us that we can trust and to which we can abandon ourselves: a sense that we are connected to others and beyond.

- *Intimacy* vs. *E-ntimacy©*: the first concept (intimacy) requires privacy, and involves self-disclosure, lowering of personal boundaries, I–Thou relationship. The second one (E-ntimacy©, typical of online relationship) involves belonging, influence, and confluence. It is based on a fantasy of similarity, perceived as normal online, and develops when two or more people agree to have a relationship without involving a body.

- *Singular* vs. *multiple self-states*: the Internet allows us to perceive and practice our different self-states without pathologising ourselves. It helps us to accept our subjectivity as a partial and polymorphous, multilayered, decentred self and to deeply integrate portrayals of self as both multiple and discontinuous, while at the same time as an integrated, continuous, unified centred self.

- *Me-ness, we-ness, and in-betweeness*: the Internet culture satisfies the need for individuality while at the same time fulfilling one's needs in relationship and the need to belong to a community and contribute to others. One can keep autonomy while belonging to an Internet group without the compromises people usually have to make when joining a community.

- *Diversity* vs. *unity*: the Internet culture allows for both a sense of diversity (where we can find a diverse expression of voices, individuals, cultures, and even languages living together) and a sense of unity at the same time (we all belong to this world-wide-web and feel a sense of connectedness to one another).

- *Small* vs. *large group*: Internet forums are a new kind of group, with some processes resembling face-to-face small groups and other dynamics resembling large groups, all the while still manifesting other psychological phenomena unique to online groups. It is a large group "in the dark" with the illusion of a small group.

- *The presence of the group leader*: this new kind of group requires forum leaders to practice a different kind of presence and dynamic administration, which includes dealing with persistent idealisation.

- *Internet forums enhance the capacity to be alone in the presence of the others*: the ability to play with the other forum members, keeping their virtual presence in mind, transforms the physical embodied group into an imagined virtual internalised group. The presence of the forum leader, including his/her idealisation as mentioned above, is crucial for members when developing this capacity.

- *Caring* vs. *intruding*: Internet groups address the dilemma of how interest in and care for others can be perceived as intrusive. Members of Internet forums are less inclined to be overly cautious, thereby isolating the suffering person, but do not go to the other extreme of forcing disclosures that violate privacy boundaries. Significant caring can develop on these forums, especially if the leader is clearly present.

- *Yalom's therapeutic factors*: most of Yalom's curative factors exist within Internet groups, contributing to the therapeutic impact of Cybergroups. They can feel cohesive and intensify hope and universality. Existential factors are amplified on the Internet because it is perceived as rising above the limitations of time and space. Participation in Internet groups can be empowering for many people.

I do not mean to ignore the dangers and threats of Internet communication. Because it lacks everything but textual cues, the Internet provides the perfect environment for massive projections. However, once we are aware of these dangers, what we do with these projections is for us to determine, as there are two polarised possibilities. One is to put the others in the position of the bad object, distort what they write in order to prove their negative hostile intentions.

This is the schizoid–paranoid position. The other is to project the ego ideal onto the others in Cyberspace and see them as all good (a manic reparation?). Of course, a realistic perception and a balanced attitude towards other people with whom we interact, keeping in mind their (hidden) subjectivity, is more beneficial than either of these extremes.

Throughout this book I explored the typical dynamics of online groups and forums. The examples and vignettes I used were taken from discussion lists, not therapy groups. It is only natural that the avid reader, who loyally followed me this far, wonders about the implications of these phenomena for online therapy groups. Although it is beyond the scope of this book to fully explore these questions, there is evidence that Internet-based therapy is growing quickly and that E-mental health can contribute to a better mental health care (for a summary of exhaustive resources, see Kenneth Pope's website about telepsychology, telehealth, & Internet-based therapy at kspope.com/ telepsychology.php, which includes 132 recent articles and many professional guidelines that focus on online counselling and Internet-based therapy). Internet-based cognitive behaviour therapy has already been tested in many trials and found to be effective in the treatment of anxiety and mood disorders (e.g., Hedman et al., 2011). The pioneering study of Barak & Wander-Schwartz from 2000 (see www.hayseed.net/MOO/JOVE/cherapy3.html), and later research (e.g., Golkaramnay, Bauer, Haug, Wolf, & Kordy, 2007) clearly show that Internet group therapy carries a lot of promise, in addition to being cost effective. Although I do not think that we could ever give up face-to-face therapeutic groups, and even though I am convinced that there is no replacement for seeing group members eye-to-eye, I do believe that online therapy groups can be effective. However, if therapists want to conduct such online groups, they should definitely know in advance what to expect, and what skills are needed. Being psychologically oriented, or even being knowledgeable about psychotherapy groups, is not enough. Online group conductors should acquire special knowledge and develop specific skills for this sophisticated and complex set of interventions. In fact, this is an *ethical imperative*, to have specialised training and/or individual or group supervision before leading an online therapy group and perhaps even a forum.

I hope that this book will be the first step in educating the therapist towards specialised training, but of course the field of online group therapy and the training of skilled online group conductors is only in its beginning stages. However, as this book was not meant to focus on the online therapy group, I do believe that after reading this book, you will become more aware of group dynamics on the Internet whether you are a therapist or not.

REFERENCES

Agazarian, Y. M. (1997). *Systems-centered Therapy for Groups*. New York: Guilford Press.

Altman, N. (2010). *The Analyst in the Inner City: Race, Class and Culture Through a Psychoanalytic Lens* (2nd edn). New York: Routledge.

Anzieu, D. (1984). *The Group and the Unconscious*. London: Routledge.

Anzieu, D. (1999). The group ego-skin. *Group Analysis, 32*: 319–329.

Argyle, M., & Dean, J. (1965). Eye-contact, distance and affiliation. *Sociometry, 28*: 289–304.

Aron, L. (1996). *A Meeting of Minds*. Hillsdale, NJ: Analytic Press.

Aron, L., & Starr, K. E. (2013). *A Psychotherapy for the People: Toward a Progressive Psychoanalysis*. New York: Routledge.

Avatar (2009). Film, directed by J. Cameron. US.

Aziz-Zadeh, L., Wilson, S. M., Rizzolatti, G., & Iacoboni, M. (2006). Congruent embodied representations for visually presented actions and linguistic phrases describing actions. *Current Biology, 16*: 1818–1823.

Barak, A. (2007). Emotional support and suicide prevention through the Internet: a field project report. *Computers in Human Behavior, 23*(2): 971–984.

Barak, A., & Grohol, J. M. (2011). Current and future trends in Internet-supported mental health interventions. *Journal of Technology in Human Services, 29*(3): 155–196.

Barak, A., & Wander-Schwartz, M. (2000). Empirical evaluation of brief group therapy conducted in an internet chat room. *Journal of Virtual Environments, 5*: www.hayseed.net/MOO/JOVE/cherapy3.html

Barratt, B. B. (1993). *Psychoanalysis and the Postmodern Impulse*. Baltimore, MD: John Hopkins University Press.

Barzilai, G. (2003). *Communities and Law: Politics and Cultures of Legal Identities*. Ann Arbor, MI: Michigan University Press.

Beck, A. P. (1981). Developmental characteristics of the system-forming process. In: J. E. Durkin (Ed.), *Living Groups: Group Psychotherapy & General System Theory* (316–332). New York: Brunner/Mazel.

Benjamin, J. (1998). *Shadow of the Other: Intersubjectivity and Gender in Psychoanalysis*. New York: Routledge.

Berman, A., Berger, M., & Gutmann, D. (2000). The division into Us and Them as a universal social structure. *Mind and Human Interaction, 11*(1): 53–72.

Bersani, L., & Phillips, A. (2008). *Intimacies*. Chicago, IL: University of Chicago Press.

Bion, W. R. (1959). *Experiences in Groups and Other Papers*. New York: Basic Books.

Bion, W. R. (1984). *Transformations*. London: Karnac.

Blackwell, D. (1994). The psyche and the system. In: D. Brown & L. Zinkin (Eds.), *The Psyche and the Social World* (pp. 27–46). London: Routledge.

Blackwell, D. (2002). The politicization of group analysis in the 21st century. *Group Analysis, 35*(1): 105–118.

Bodley, J. H. (1994). *Cultural Anthropology: Tribes, States, and the Global System*. New York: McGraw Hill.

Brewer, N. B. (1991). The social self: on being the same and different at the same time. *Personality and Social Psychology Bulletin, 17*: 475–482.

Bromberg, P. M. (1996). Standing in the spaces: the multiplicity of self and the psychoanalytic relationship. *Contemporary Psychoanalysis, 32*: 509–535.

Brown, D. (1994). Self development through subjective interaction. A fresh look at "Ego Training on Action". In: D. Brown & L. Zinkin (Eds.), *The Psyche and the Social World* (pp. 80–98). London: Routledge.

Brown, D. (2001). A contribution to the understanding of the social unconscious. *Group Analysis, 34*(1): 29–38

Brown, D., & Zinkin, L. (Eds.) (1994). *The Psyche and the Social World*. London: Routledge.

Buckley, W. (1967). *Sociology and Modern Systems Theory*. Englewood Cliffs, NJ: Prentice-Hall.

Burman, E. (2002). Gender, sexuality and power in groups. *Group Analysis*, 35(4): 540–559.

Burman, E. (2004). Organising for change? Group-analytic perspectives on a feminist action research project. *Group Analysis*, 37(1): 91–108.

Carrithers, M. (1992). *Why Humans Have Cultures: Explaining Anthropology and Social Diversity*. Oxford: Oxford University Press.

Christopher, J. C. (2001). Culture and psychotherapy: toward a hermeneutic approach. *Psychotherapy*, 38(2): 115–128.

Cohen, B. D. (2002). Groups to resolve conflicts between groups: diplomacy with a therapeutic dimension. *Group*, 26(3): 189–204.

Cohen, B. D., Ettin, M. F., & Fidler, J. W. (1998). Conceptions of leadership: the "analytic stance" of the group psychotherapist. *Group Dynamics: Theory, Research, & Practice*, 2: 118–131.

Cohen, B. D., Ettin, M. F., & Fidler, J. W. (Eds.) (2002). *Group Psychotherapy and Political Reality: A Two-Way Mirror*. Madison, CT: International Universities Press

Cole, M. (1996). *Cultural Psychology*. Cambridge, MA: Harvard University Press.

Corey, G. (1994). *Theory and Practice of Group Counseling*. Pacific Grove, CA: Brooks/Cole.

Correa De Jesus, N. (1999). Genealogies of the self in virtual-geographical reality. In: A. J. Gordo-Lopez & I. Parker (Eds.), *Cyberpsychology* (pp. 77–91). Houndmills: Macmillan Press.

Cozolino, L. (2006). *The Neuroscience of Human Relationships: Attachment and the Developing Social Brain*. New York: Norton.

Csikszentmihalyi, M. (1990). *Flow: The Psychology of Optimal Experience*. New York: Harper & Row.

Dalal, F. (1998). *Taking the Group Seriously: Towards a Post-Foulkesian Group Analytic Theory*. London: Jessica Kingsley.

Dalal, F. (2001). The social unconscious: a post-Foulkesian perspective. *Group Analysis*, 34(4): 539–555.

Davidson, B. (1998). The internet and the large group. *Group Analysis*, 31(4): 457–471.

Davies, J. (2006). "Hello Newbie! big welcome hugs hope u like it here as much as I do!": an exploration of teenagers informal online learning. In: D. Buckingham & R.W. Mahwah (Eds.), *Digital Generations: Children, Young People and New Media* (pp. 211–229). New-Jersey and London: Lawrence Erlbaum.

de Maré, P. (1975). The politics of large groups. In: L. Kreeger (Ed.), *The Large Group: Dynamics and Therapy*. London: Constable.

de Maré, P., Piper, R., & Thompson, S. (1991). *Koinonia: From Hate through Dialogue, to Culture in the Large Group*. London: Karnac.

Derrida, J. (1974). *Of Grammatology*. Baltimore, MD: John Hopkins University Press.

Eagle, M. N., & Wolitzky, D. L. (1992). Psychoanalytic theories of psychotherapy. In: D. K. Friedheim (Ed.), *History of Psychotherapy: A Century of Change* (pp. 109–158). Washington, DC: American Psychological Association.

Elias, N. (1978). *The Civilizing Process*. Oxford: Basil Blackwell.

Elias, N. (1989). *Theory, Culture, Society*. London: Sage.

Elias, N. (1991). *The Symbol Theory*. London: Sage.

Erikson, E. H. (1950). *Childhood and Society*. New York: Norton.

Ettin, M. F., Cohen, B. D., & Fidler, J. W. (1997). Group-as-a-whole theory viewed in its 20th century context. *Group Dynamics: Theory, Research & Practice, 1*: 329–340.

Fehr, S. S. (1999). *Introduction to Group Therapy: A Practical Guide*. New York: Haworth Press.

Finn, J. (1999). An exploration of helping processes in an online self-help group focusing on issues of disability. *Health & Social Work, 24*: 220–232.

Foguel, B. S. (1994). The group experienced as mother: early psychic structures in analytic groups. *Group Analysis, 27*: 265–285.

Foster, R. (1992). Psychoanalysis and the bilingual patient: some observations on the influence of language choice on the transference. *Psychoanalytic Psychology, 9*(1): 61–76.

Foulkes, S. H. (1948). *Introduction to Group Analytic Psychotherapy*. London: Heinemann.

Foulkes, S. H. (1964). *Therapeutic Group Analysis*. London: Allen and Unwin [reprinted London: Karnac, 1984].

Foulkes, S. H. (Ed.) (1967). *Group Analysis International Panel and Correspondence*. London: Group Analytic Society.

Foulkes, S. H. (1973). The group as matrix of the individual's mental life. In: L. R. Wolberg & E. K. Schwartz (Eds.), *Group Therapy 1973—An Overview*. New York: Intercontinental Medical Book Corporation.

Foulkes, S. H. (1975). *Group Analytic Psychotherapy, Method and Principles*. London: Gordon & Breach.

Foulkes, S. H. (1990). *Selected Papers: Psychoanalysis and Group Analysis*. London: Karnac.

Foulkes, S. H., & Anthony, E. J. (1965). *Group Psychotherapy: the Psychoanalytic Approach*. Harmondsworth: Penguin [reprinted London: Karnac, 1984].

Freud, S. (1921c). *Group Psychology and the Analysis of the Ego. S.E., 18*: 65–144. London: Hogarth.

Freud, S. (1930a). *Civilisation and Its Discontents. S.E., 21*: 57–146. London: Hogarth.

Frosh, S. (1999). *The Politics of Psychoanalysis: An Introduction to Freudian and Post-Freudian Theory* (2nd edn). New York: New York University Press.

Gantt, S. P. (2012). Functional subgrouping and the systems-centered approach to group therapy. In: J. L. Kleinberg (Ed.), *The Wiley-Blackwell Handbook of Group Psychotherapy* (pp. 113–137). New York: John Wiley & Sons.

Gerson, S. (2004). The relational unconscious: a core element of intersubjectivity, thirdness, and clinical process. *Psychoanalytic Quarterly, 73*: 63–98.

Ghent, E. (1999). Masochism, submission, surrender: masochism as a perversion of surrender. In: S. A. Mitchell & L. Aron (Eds.), *Relational Psychoanalysis: The Emergence of a Tradition*, (pp. 211–243). Hillsdale, NJ: Analytic Press.

Gods Must Be Crazy, The (1980). Film, directed by J. Uys. South Africa.

Golkaramnay, V., Bauer, S., Haug, S., Wolf, M., & Kordy, H. (2007). The exploration of the effectiveness of group therapy through an Internet chat as aftercare: a controlled naturalistic study. *Psychotherapy & Psychosomatics, 76*: 219–225.

Greetz, C. (1973). *The Interpretation of Cultures*. New York: Basic Books.

Guigon, C. B. (1993). Authenticity, moral values and psychotherapy. In: C. B. Guigon (Ed.), *The Cambridge Companion to Heidegger*, (pp. 215–239). Cambridge: Cambridge University Press.

Halbwachs, M. (1980). *The Collective Memory*. New York: Harper & Row Colophon.

Hall, E. T. (1976). *Beyond Culture*. New York: Doubleday.

Haraway, D. (1985). Manifesto for cyborgs: science, technology, and social feminism in the 1980s. *Socialist Review, 80*: 65–108.

Hedman, E., Andersson, G., Andersson, E., Ljótsson, B., Rück, C., Asmundson, G. J. G., & Lindefors, N. (2011). Internet-based cognitive-behavioural therapy for severe health anxiety: randomised controlled trial, *British Journal of Psychiatry, 198*(3): 230–236.

Hill, R. (1972). Modern system theory and the family: a confrontation. *Social Science Information, 10*(5): 7–26.

Hinshelwood, R. D. (1999). How Foulksian was Bion? *Group Analysis, 32*: 469–488.

Hofstede, G. (2001). *Culture's Consequences: Comparing Values, Behaviors, Institutions, and Organizations Across Nations*. Thousand Oaks, CA: Sage.

Holland, N. (1996). The Internet regression. [Online]. In: J. Suler (Ed.), *Psychology of Cyberspace*. Available at www.rider.edu/~suler/ psycyber/holland.html. [Retrieved 26 December, 2011].

Hopper, E. (1996). The social unconscious in clinical work. *Group, 20*(1): 7–42.

Hopper, E. (1997). Traumatic experience in the unconscious life of groups: a fourth basic assumption. *Group Analysis, 30*: 439–470.

Hopper, E. (2001). The social unconscious: theoretical considerations. *Group Analysis, 34*: 9–27.

Hopper, E. (2003). *The Social Unconscious: Selected Papers*. London: Jessica Kingsley.

Hopper, E. (2009). The theory of the basic assumption of incohesion: aggregation/massification of (ba) I:A/M. *British Journal of Psychotherapy, 25*(2): 214–229.

Hopper, E., & Weinberg, H. (Eds.) (2011). *The Social Unconscious in Persons, Groups, and Societies: Volume 1: Mainly Theory*. London: Karnac.

Hunt, J. (1989). *Psychoanalytic Aspects of Fieldwork*. London: Sage.

Iacoboni, M. (2008). *Mirroring People: The New Science of How We Connect With Others*. New York: Farrar, Straus, & Giroux.

Irwin-Zarecka, I. (1994). *Frames of Remembrance: The Dynamics of Collective Memory*. Piscataway, NJ: Transaction.

Jacobson, L. (1989). The group as an object in the cultural field. *International Journal of Group Psychotherapy, 39*(4): 475–497.

Jacoby, R. (1975). *Social Amnesia: A Critique of Comtemporary Psychology from Adler to Laing*. New York: Beacon.

Jones, S. G. (1997). The internet and its social landscape. In: S. G. Jones (Ed.), *Virtual Culture, Identity and Communication in Cybersociety* (pp. 7–35). London: Sage.

Jost, J. T. (1997). An experimental replication of the depressed entitlement effect among women. *Psychology of Women Quarterly, 21*: 387–393.

Jung, C. G. (1934). The archetypes and the collective unconscious. In: *Collected Papers Vol. 9, Part 1*. London: Routledge & Kegan Paul.

Kaës, R. (1987). La Troisième Difference. *Revue de Psychotherapie Psychoanalytique de Groupe, 9–10*: 5–30.

Karterud, S. (1998). The group self, empathy, intersubjectivity and hermeneutics: a group analytic perspective. In: I. Harwood & M. Pines (Eds.), *Self Experiences in Group: Intersubjective and Self Psychological*

Pathways to Human Understanding (pp. 83–98). London: Jessica Kingsley.

Kernberg, O. F. (1989). The temptations of conventionality. *International Review of Psycho-Analysis, 16*: 191–205.

Knauss, W. (2006). The group in the unconscious—a bridge between the individual and the society. *Group Analysis, 39*(2): 159–170.

Kohut, H. (1971). *The Analysis of the Self.* London: Hogarth Press.

Kraut, R., Kiesler, S., Boneva, B., Cummings, J., Helgeson, V., & Crawford, A. (2002). Internet paradox revisited. *Journal of Social Issues, 58*(1): 49–74.

Kraut, R., Patterson, M., Lundmark, V., Kiesler, S., Mukopadhyay, T., & Scherlis, W. (1998). Internet paradox: a social technology that reduces social involvement and psychological well-being? *American Psychologist, 53*(9): 1017–1031.

Kreeger, L. (Ed.) (1975). *The Large Group: Dynamics and Therapy.* London: Karnac.

Kulka, R. (1991). Reflections on the future of self-psychology and its role in the evolution of psychoanalysis. In: A. Goldberg (Ed.), *The Evolution of Self-sychology: Progress in Self-psychology, Vol. 7* (pp. 175–183). Hillsdale, NJ: Analytic Press.

Lacan, J. (1977). *Ecirts: a Selection* (A. Sheridan, trans.). New York & London: Norton.

Lather, P. (1991). *Feminist Research in Education: Within/Against.* Geelong, Victoria: Deakin University Press.

Lauren, S. E. (2002). Special issue: a group analysis of class, status groups and inequality. *Group Analysis, 35*(3): 339–341.

Lawrence, G. W., Bain, A., & Gould, L. J. (1996). The fifth basic assumption. *Free Associations, 6*(37): 28–55 [reprinted in *Tongue With Fire: Groups in Experience.* London: Karnac, 2000].

Le Roy, J. (1994). Group analysis and culture. In: D. Brown & L. Zinkin (Eds.), *The Psyche and the Social World* (pp. 180–201). London: Routledge.

Leibniz, G. W. (1765/1896). *New Essays Concerning Human Understanding.* (A. G. Langley, trans.) New York: Macmillan.

Leonetti, I. T. (1992). From multicultural to intercultural: is it necessary to move from one to the other? In: J. Lynch, C. Modgil, & S. Modgil (Eds.), *Cultural Diversity in the Schools* (pp. 153–156). London: Falmer Press.

Lévinas, E. (1984). Ethics of the infinite. In: R. Kearney (Ed.), *Dialogues With Contemporary Continental Thinkers* (pp. 47–69). Manchester:

Manchester University Press [reprinted in R. Cohen (Ed.), *Face to Face with Lévinas* (pp. 13–33). Albany: Suny Press, 1986].

Liebert, T. W., Smith-Adcock, S., & Munson, J. (2008). Exploring how online self-help groups compares to face-to-face groups from the user perspective. *Journal of Technology in Counseling*, 5(1). Retrieved 30 December 2012 from jtc.columbusstate.edu/Vol5_1/Leibert.htm.

Livingstone, S., Haddon, L., Görzig, A., & Ólafsson, K. (2011). *Risks and Safety on the Internet: The Perspective of European Children. Full Findings*. LSE, London: EU Kids Online. Retrieved 25 November 2011. www.eukidsonline.net

Lombard, M., & Ditton, T. (1997). At the heart of it all: the concept of presence. *Journal of Computer-Mediated Communication*, 3(2). Reteieved 10 October 2011 from www.ascusc.org/jcmc/vol3/issue2/lombard.html

MacKenzie, K. R. (1997). *Time Managed Group Psychotherapy: Effective Clinical Applications*. Washington, DC: American Psychiatric Press.

MacKenzie, K. R., & Livesley, W. J. (1983). A developmental model for brief group therapy. In: R. R. Dies & K. R. MacKenzie (Eds.), *Advances in Group Psychotherapy: Integrating Research and Practice* (pp. 101–116). New York: International University Press.

Mahler, M. S., Pine, F., & Bergman, A. (1975). *The Psychological Birth Of The Human Infant*. New York: Basic Books.

Mantovani, G., & Riva, G. (1999). "Real" presence: how different ontologies generate different criteria for presence, telepresence and virtual presence. *Presence*, 8(5): 540–550.

Matrix, The (1999). Film, directed by A. Wachowski & L. Wachowski. USA.

McKenna, K. Y. A., & Green, A. S. (2002). Virtual group dynamics. *Group Dynamics*, 6(1): 116–127.

McKenna, K. Y. A., Green, A. S., & Gleason, M. E. J. (2002). Relationship formation on the Internet: what's the big attraction? *Journal of Social Issues*, 58(1): 9–31.

Mead, G. H. (1968). The genesis of the self. In: C. Gordon & K. Gergen (Eds.), *The Self in Social Interaction* (pp. 51–59). New York: Wiley.

Minuchin, S. (1974). *Families and Family Therapy*. Cambridge, MA: Harvard University Press.

Mitchell, S. A. (1993). *Hope and Dread in Psychoanalysis*. New York: Basic Books.

Mitchell, S. A. (2002). *Can Love Last? The Fate of Romance Over Time*. New York: Norton.

Moreno, J. L. (1934/1978). *Who Shall Survive?: Foundations of Sociometry, Group Psychotherapy, and Sociodrama* (3rd edn). New York: Beacon House.

Nitsun, M. (1996). *The Anti-group: Destructive Forces in the Group and Their Creative Potential*. London: Routledge.

Oldenquist, A. (1988). An explanation of retribution. *Journal of Philosophy*, 41: 464–478.

Ormont, L. R. (1992). *The Group Therapy Experience*. New York: St. Martin's Press.

Ormont, L. R. (1996). The group as agent of change. In: L. B. Furgeri (Ed.), *The Technique of Group Treatment: the Collected Papers of Louis Ormont* (pp. 37–45). Madison, CT: Psychosocial Press, 2001.

Parker, I. (1997). *Psychoanalytic Culture: Psychoanalytic Discourse in Western Society*. London: Sage.

Perron, B. (2002). Online support for caregivers of people with a mental illness. *Psychiatric Rehabilitation Journal*, 26: 70–77.

Perry, P. (2001). White means never having to say you're ethnic. *Journal of Contemporary Ethnography*, 30: 56–91.

Phoenix, A. (1987). Theories of gender and black families. In: G. Weiner & A. Amot (Eds.), *Gender Under Scrutiny* (pp. 16–50). London: Hutchinson.

Pines, M. (1981). The frame of reference of group psychotherapy. *International Journal of Group Psychotherapy*, 31(3): 275–285.

Pines, M. (2002). The coherency of group analysis. *Group Analysis*, 35(1): 13–26.

Pines, M. (2003). Large groups and culture. In: S. Schneider & H. Weinberg (Eds.), *The Large Group Revisited: The Herd, Primal Horde, Crowds and Masses* (pp. 44–57). London: Jessica Kingsley.

Plant, S. (1997). *Zeroes + Ones: Digital Women and the New Technoculture*. New York: Doubleday.

Polak, M. (2006). It's a URL thing: community versus commodity in girl-focused netscape. In: D. Buckingham & R.W. Mahwah (Eds.), *Digital Generations: Children, Young People and New Media* (pp. 177–193). New Jersey and London: Lawrence Erlbaum.

Pope, C., Ziebland, S., & Mays, N. (2000). Qualitative research in health care: analysing qualitative data. *British Medical Journal*, 320: 114–116.

Powell, A. (1991). The embodied matrix: discussion on paper by Romano Fiumara. *Group Analysis*, 24: 419–423.

Prilleltensky, A. (1989). Psychology and the status quo. *American Psychologist*, 44: 795–802.

Raufman, R., & Ben-Cnaan R. (2009). Red Riding Hood—text, hypertext and context in an Israeli nationalistic internet forum. *Journal of Folklore Research*, 46(1): 43–66.

Raufman, R., & Milo, H. (in press). The princess in the wooden-body: oral Israeli versions of the maiden in the chest in light of incest victims' blogs. *Journal of American Folklore*.

Ridley, M. (1996). *The Origins of Virtue*. London: Viking.

Rifkin, J. (2009). *The Empathic Civilization: The Race to Global Consciousness in a World in Crisis*. New York: Penguin.

Rippa, B., Moss, E., & Chirurg, M. (2011). Observations on the interplay between large and small analytic groups. *Group Analysis*, 44(4): 439–453.

Roberts, J., & Pines, M. (Eds.) (1991). *The Practice of Group Analysis*. London and New York: Tavistock/Routledge.

Rogers, C. R. (1957). The necessity and sufficient of therapeutic personality change. *Journal of Consulting Psychology*, 21: 95–103.

Rogoff, B. (2003). *The Cultural Nature of Human Development*. New York: Oxford University Press.

Rose, S. (1997). *Lifeline*. London: Penguin.

Rutan, S. J., Stone, N. W., & Shay, J. (2007). *Psychodynamic Group Psychotherapy* (4th edn). New York: Guilford Press

Safran, J. D. (2006). The relational unconscious, the American enchanted interior and the return of the repressed. *Contemporary Psychoanalysis*, 42: 393–412.

Salem, D. A., Bogat, G. A., & Reid, C. (1997). Mutual help goes on-line. *The Journal of Community Psychology*, 25: 189–207.

Sampson, E. E. (1989). The deconstruction of the self. In: K. J. Gerken & J. Shotter (Eds.), *Texts of Identity* (pp. 1–19). London: Sage.

Sarason, S. B. (1985). And what is the public interest? *American Psychologist*, 41(8): 889–905.

Scharff, J. (Ed.) (2013). *Psychoanalysis Online*. London: Karnac.

Scheidlinger, S. (1974). On the concept of the "mother-group". *International Journal of Group Psychotherapy*, 24: 417–428.

Schermer, V. L. (2010). Mirror neurons: their implications for group psychotherapy. *International Journal of Group Psychotherapy*, 60(4): 487–513.

Schiff, S. B., & Glassman, S. M. (1969). Large and small group therapy in a state mental health centre. *International Journal of Group Psychotherapy*, 19: 150–157.

Schloerb, D. W. (1995). A quantitative measure of telepresence. *Presence: Teleoperators and Virtual Environments*, 4: 64–80.

Schneider S., & Weinberg H. (Eds.) (2003). *The Large Group Revisited: The Herd, Primal Horde, Crowds and Masses*. London: Jessica Kingsley.

Scholz, R. (2011). The foundation matrix and the social unconscious. In: E. Hopper & H. Weinberg (Eds.), *The Social Unconscious in Persons, Groups, and Societies: Volume 1: Mainly Theory* (pp. 265–285). London: Karnac.

Schulte, P. (2000). Holding in mind: intersubjectivity, subject relations and the group. *Group Analysis, 33*(4): 531–544.

Segalla, R. A. (1996). The unbearable embeddedness of being. *Group, 20*: 257–271.

Sengun, S. (2001). Migration as a transitional space and group analysis. *Group Analysis, 34*: 65–78.

Sey, J. (1999). The labouring body and the posthuman. In: A. J. Gordo-Lopez & I. Parker (Eds.), *Cyberpsychology* (pp. 25–41). Houndmills: Macmillan.

Shapira, I. (2010). Texting generation doesn't share boomers' taste for talk. *Washington Post*. Retrievede 15 March 2012 from www.washington post.com/wp-dyn/content/article/2010/08/07/AR2010080702848. html

Shields, R. (Ed.) (1996). *Cultures of Internet: Virtual Spaces, Real Histories, Living Bodies*. London: Sage.

Sidanius, J., & Prato, F. (1999). *Social Dominance: An Intergroup Theory of Social Hierarchy and Oppression*. New York: Cambridge University Press.

Stacey, R. (2000). Reflexivity, self-organization and emergence in the group matrix. *Group Analysis, 33*(4): 501–514.

Stern, D. (1985). *The Interpersonal World of the Infant: A View from Psychoanalysis and Development*. New York: Basic Books.

Stone, W. N. (2005). The group-as-a-whole: self-psychological perspective. *Group: The Journal of the Eastern Group Psychotherapy Society, 29*(2): 239–256.

Strozier. C. B. (Ed.) (1985). *Self Psychology and the Humanities*. New York & London: Norton.

Suler, J. (1996). Transference among people online. Retrieved 25 November 2011 from the World Wide Web: users.rider.edu/~suler/ psycyber/transference.html

Suler, J. (1999). Cyberspace as psychological space. Retrieved 25 November 2011 from the World Wide Web: users.rider.edu/~suler/ psycyber/psychspace.html

Taylor, D. M. (2002). *The Quest for Identity: From Minority Groups to Generation Xers*. Westport, CT: Praeger.

Taylor, S. E. (1989). *Positive Illusions: Creative Self-Deception and the Healthy Mind*. New York: Basic Books.

Tubert-Oklander, J. (2006). I, thou, and us: relationality and the interpretive process. *Psychoanalytic Dialogues, 16*: 199–216.

Tuckman, B. W. (1965). Developmental sequence in small groups. *Psychological Bulletin, 63*: 384–399.

Turkle, S. (1995). *Life on the Screen: Identity in the Age of the Internet*. New York: Simon & Schuster.

Turkle, S. (2011). *Alone Together: Why We Expect More From Technology and Less From Each Other*. New York: Basic Books.

Turner, J. C., Hogg, M. A., Oakes, P. J., Reicher, S. D., & Wetherell, M. S. (1987). *Rediscovering the Social Group. A Self-categorizing Theory*. Oxford: Basol Blackwell.

Turquet, P. (1974). Leadership—the individual and the group. In: G. S. Gibbard, J. J. Hartman & R. D. Mann (Eds.). *Analyses of Groups* (pp. 87–144). San Francisco & London: Jossey Bass.

Turquet, P. (1975). Threats to identity in the large group. In: L. Kreeger (Ed.), *The Large Group: Dynamics and Therapy* (pp. 87–144). London: Karnac.

Twenge, J. M., & Campbell, W. K. (2009). *The Narcissism Epidemic: Living in the Age of Entitlement*. New York: Fine Press.

Van der Kleij, G. (1983). The setting of the group. *Group Analysis, 16*(1): 75–80.

Volkan, V. (2001). Transgenerational transmissions and chosen traumas: an aspect of large group identity. *Group Analysis, 34*: 79–97.

Von Bertalanffy, L. (1956). General system theory. *General Systems, 1*(1): 11–17.

Wainwright, D. (1997). Can sociological research be qualitative, critical and valid? *The Qualitative Report* [On-line serial], *3*(2). Available at www.nova.edu/ssss/QR/QR3-2/wain.html

Walshe, J. (1995). The external space in group work. *Group Analysis, 28*: 413–427.

Weinberg, H. (2001). Group process and group phenomena on the Internet. *International Journal of Group Psychotherapy, 51*(3): 361–379.

Weinberg, H. (2002). Community unconscious on the Internet. *Group Analysis, 35*(1): 165–183.

Weinberg, H. (2003a). The culture of the group and groups from different cultures. *Group Analysis, 36*(2): 253–268.

Weinberg, H. (2003b). The large group in a virtual environment. In: S. Schneider & H. Weinberg (Eds.), *The Large Group Revisited: The Herd, Primal Horde, Crowds and Masses* (pp. 188–200). London: Jessica Kingsley.

Weinberg, H. (2006). Regression in the group revisited. *Group: The Journal of the Eastern Group Psychotherapy Society, 30*(1): 1–17.

Weinberg, H. (2007). So what is this social unconscious anyway? *Group Analysis, 40*(3): 307–322.

Weinberg, H., & Schneider, S. (2003). Introduction: background, structure and dynamics of the large group. In: S. Schneider & H. Weinberg (Eds.), *The Large Group Revisited: The Herd, Primal Horde, Crowds and Masses* (pp. 13–26). London: Jessica Kingsley.

Weinberg, H., & Toder, M. (2004). The hall of mirrors in small, large, and virtual groups. *Group Analysis, 37*(4): 492–507.

Weinberg, H., & Weishut, D. J. N. (2012). The large group: dynamics, social implications and therapeutic value. In: J. L. Kleinberg (Ed.), *The Wiley-Blackwell Handbook of Group Psychotherapy* (pp.457–479). West Sussex: Wiley-Blackwell.

Weinberg, N., Uken, J. S., Schmale, J., & Adamek, M. (1995). Therapeutic factors: their presence in a computer-mediated support group. *Social Work with Groups, 18*(4): 57–69.

Williamson, J. (1988). *Decoding Advertisements*. London: Marion Boyars.

Winnicott, D. W. (1958). The capacity to be alone. *International Journal of Psycho-Analysis, 39*: 416–420.

Winnicott, D. W. (1986). *Holding and Interpretation: Fragment of an Analysis*. New York: Basic Books.

Winnicott, D. W. (1987). *The Maturational Process and the Facilitating Environment*. London: Hogarth.

Yalom, I. D. (1970). *The Theory and Practice of Group Psychotherapy* (1st edn). New York: Basic Books.

Yalom, I. D. (1995). *The Theory and Practice of Group Psychotherapy* (4th edn). New York: Basic Books.

Yalom, I. D., & Leszcz, M. (2005). *The Theory and Practice of Group Psychotherapy* (5th edn). New York: Basic Books.

Yogev, H. (2012). The development of empathy and group analysis. *Group Analysis, 46*(1): 61–80.

Zerubavel, A. (2003). *Time Maps: Collective Memory and the Social Shape of the Past*. Chicago, IL: Chicago University Press.

INDEX